Supernatural
Arkansas

*Ghosts, Monsters, and
the Unexplained*

Alan Lowe and Jason Hall

Schiffer®
Publishing Ltd

4880 Lower Valley Road • Atglen, PA 19310

Copyright © 2012 by Alan Lowe and Jason Hall
Library of Congress Control Number: 2012938682

Designed by Danielle D. Farmer
Type set in Tiza Negra/NewBskvll BT

ISBN: 978-0-7643-4123-6
Printed in China

Schiffer Books are available at special discounts for bulk purchases for sales promotions or premiums. Special editions, including personalized covers, corporate imprints, and excerpts can be created in large quantities for special needs. For more information contact the publisher:

Published by Schiffer Publishing, Ltd.
4880 Lower Valley Road
Atglen, PA 19310
Phone: (610) 593-1777; Fax: (610) 593-2002
E-mail: Info@schifferbooks.com

For the largest selection of fine reference books on this and related subjects, please visit our website at **www.schifferbooks.com**
We are always looking for people to write books on new and related subjects. If you have an idea for a book, please contact us at proposals@schifferbooks.com

This book may be purchased from the publisher.
Please try your bookstore first.
You may write for a free catalog.

In Europe, Schiffer books are distributed by
Bushwood Books
6 Marksbury Ave.
Kew Gardens
Surrey TW9 4JF England
Phone: 44 (0) 20 8392 8585; Fax: 44 (0) 20 8392 9876
E-mail: info@bushwoodbooks.co.uk
Website: www.bushwoodbooks.co.uk

Acknowledgments

Jason and I made many new friends during the process of researching and writing *Supernatural Arkansas: Ghosts, Monsters, and the Unexplained.*

We would like to thank each one who contributed their time, talents, and stories while helping us uncover the facts contained in this book.

The following people provided Jason and me with valuable information: Lee McLane, *Popular Science Magazine*, Spirit Seekers Paranormal Investigation Research & Intervention Team (SPIRIT), and The Arkansas Game and Fish Commission. Thanks to Angela Turney, Gary Ivy, Violet Renee, and Robin White for providing photographs and artwork. We want to give a special thanks to Angie for giving us the inspiration we needed to keep us on course, for putting up with our individualism, and for being a friend when we needed one.

Some locations in this book require permission to visit. Always follow local laws concerning trespassing.

Contents

by Jason Hall
FOREWORD

Alan Lowe and I wrote this book as a follow up to *The Ghosts of Little Rock: Tales of the City's Most Haunted Places*. We received significant positive feedback; and one of the most repeated questions was, "What about the rest of the State?" Arkansas is known for its natural beauty and popular tourist destinations. Many people are not aware of the darker side, the side that lurks unseen in the night, the side where the dead come back to life, where aliens perform experimental medical procedures on abducted human species, and monsters crawl out from the shadows and into your nightmares. We reveal those stories in *Supernatural Arkansas: Ghosts, Monsters, and the Unexplained*.

As paranormal investigators with the Spirit Seekers Paranormal Investigation Research & Intervention Team (SPIRIT), we have visited many of these sites, and share our experiences with you. Some stories in this book have been passed down from generation to generation, some have made headlines. Still others haunt the minds of those who have experienced Arkansas's dark side firsthand. You are invited to explore some of the most shadowy corners of the state as the stories unfold and the shadows start to talk to you.

In the most comprehensive guide of its kind, we will lead you on a journey that will require you to open your mind and see what most choose to ignore. Discover the haunted courthouse in Desha County, and the monster that resides in Lake Conway. Hear how the ghost of one lonely little boy waits for the father who never came in Lamar, Arkansas. Ride along as we take you down the Gurdon railroad tracks to see the Ghost Light. Join us for many more adventures through the mysterious recesses of Arkansas.

There is another side to life and death. There is a middle-place where spirits that have left this world reside and watch over us. There are creatures roaming the state that defy modern science. Only some of them are of this earth.

After taking this journey with us, you will know that sometimes the dead do come back, and sometimes, the creaking you hear under your bed at night is not just the settling of the house.

The Mississippi River, as the road disappears into waters. Jason and I had to do a little walking to dueling grounds and the actual grounds were They can be seen to the extreme left of th

by Alan Lowe
PREFACE (Back roads)

Co-Founder and Lead Investigator, Spirit Seekers of Arkansas

Welcome to the *Supernatural Arkansas*, Jason and I would like to thank you for selecting our book on supernatural happenings in this haunted state. As far as we know, this book is the first of its kind to address our state's ghosts, monsters, and the unexplained as seen by many Arkansas citizens. Jason and I have listened to hundreds of stories and met many interesting people across the State while researching and writing this book. As the book developed and our publisher took note of it is potential, we were asked to take pictures of all the hot spots covered in this volume. In the process, we encountered some of our biggest adventures to date.

To get to some of the locations, we tried shortcuts given to us by locals along the way. As we traveled one-lane, tree-lined county roads, we imagined echoes of *dueling banjos*. Mother Nature tried her best to keep us at home. In spite of torrential rains, flooded creeks, washed out roads, tornadoes, and our overactive imaginations, we really enjoyed getting out and meeting our fellow Arkys on their home turf. Arkansans are, by far, some of the most interesting and colorful people that we have ever met. We hope you will enjoy all of the great stories and pictures that we present to you.

Two years ago, when we started research for our first book, we discovered that there were many more untold stories that people were ready to share. Our team of investigators had been to the sites of many popular stories, but there were still more cases that were just as exciting and waiting to be discovered.

We decided to concentrate on all aspects of the paranormal tales in Arkansas. There were ghost stories, such as the Mena Poltergeist where Ed Shinn and his wife, Birdie, along with their fifteen-year-old grandson, Charles Shaeffer, were run out of their home by an unseen, angry spirit. Or, the Old Washington Jail Bed and Breakfast where the Sheriff of Nevada County was incarcerated for a crime against his family, but rather than be judged, he hung himself; and now he roams the halls rattling doorknobs ensuring all is well. We ran across stories of monsters, such as the great and fierce Gowrow Monster of northern Searcy County that is known to feed on livestock and young children alike; and the legendary Fouke Monster, known to attack people without warning. Many stories of unexplained flying objects were told to us as well, such as the kidnapping of Lisa in Searcy where the aliens experimented on her before explaining why they picked her out of the hundreds of other locals; or the airships that have been reported around Hot Springs as far back as 1897 when the strange people landed and offered rides to the locals.

All of these stories and more have given Jason and me a clear understanding of why Arkansas is the *Natural State* by day and the *Supernatural State* after the sun goes down. We hope that our stories will give you a better understanding of Arkansas history. All in all, we believe Arkansas to be one of the most haunted states in America.

Now, come along with us as we take you through the haunted backwoods to destinations where only a few have dared to go. Thanks so much and Sweet Screams.

The White River out of its banks. We were close to Jacksonport looking for "Whitie" or the White River Monster. We finally got the shot we were looking for but, once again, we had to park and wade to our destination.

The End of Time

Beebe, Arkansas

On the morning of January 1, 2011, thousands of Red-Winged Blackbirds littered the yards, rooftops, and roadways of Bebee. Witnesses commented that the birds looked as if they had flown into an invisible wall. They were flying one minute, then stopped and dropped to the ground, dead. *Photo courtesy of* Lee McLane-Ed/ Pub., The Beebe News.

Thunder snow, Christmas tornadoes, floods, earthquakes, thousands of birds dropping dead from the sky, and thousands of fish dying un-natural deaths in the same short stretch of river means what to local residents of north central Arkansas? If a person was to listen to and believe government officials, it means nothing. On a wet 2011 New Years Eve in Beebe, Arkansas, the fact that thousands of red-winged black birds all died while in mid flight and rained down on the small community of Beebe was no big deal. As a matter of fact, they said that it happens all the time. Somehow these massive deaths of wildlife rarely get reported to the general public. Officials with the Arkansas Game and Fish say that it was only reported this time because it happened in a populated area. But yet as the sun came up in Beebe, cleanup crews wearing protective suits, gas masks, and rubber gloves spent the holiday weekend gathering the carcasses.

There are people who believe that this is the start of the end. Doomsday enthusiasts are reveling in the media attention that the end of times predictions are real. What could have caused so many birds to drop from the sky is anybody's guess. Several theories exist that are all very interesting and have been delivered by credible authorities.

Cannons

The weather had been stormy prior to sunset as a cold front was ripping through the state. The rain had stopped, but the skies remained cloudy with a threat of more rain. The foul weather did not stop the traditional New Year's Eve celebrations that country folk enjoy. At the stroke of midnight, it is not uncommon to hear your friends and neighbors discharging firearms into the air. Beebe is a farming community, and, in the past, have had trouble raising crops because of the wildlife that lives in the woods surrounding the farms. The farmers have developed a system to keep pesky birds from devouring their crops. They use a propane-powered air cannon. It is set on a timer to start firing puffs of air at set intervals from just after sundown to a little before sunup. After sundown the birds go to roost in nearby trees. The puffs of air are harmless in most cases but can be nerve racking until a person gets use to it. Birds and other wildlife rarely get used to the noise.

On New Year's Eve, the farmers have been known to fire these cannons, rather than their guns, to stay out of trouble with the local law. This celebration was no different and the farmers had been firing the cannons. When the cannons are fired at night, the birds will leave their roost and fly to the next area with trees, causing the birds at the new location to move somewhere else, causing a domino effect. This is considered by most to be the underlying reason that the birds were up and flying.

Fireworks

The bird carcasses were cleaned up on January 1. Seventeen of the bodies were sent to out-of-state labs in Georgia and Wisconsin. The Arkansas State officials speculated that the birds had been scared into flight by fireworks or the air cannons and were flying at low levels, crashing into trees, farm structures, and parked automobiles. This was the cause of their death, or at least that is what Arkansas Fish and Game officials wanted us to believe.

Blunt-Force Trauma

The initial toxicology reports returned negative. The birds had not died due to any form of disease or poison. The necropsies that were conducted by the out-of-state labs indicated that the birds had died of blunt-force trauma. This is exactly what the local officials had been saying all along, but now they had independent scientists from two outside sources to verify their findings.

There was only one problem with this conclusion. The lab scientists' report from Georgia and Wisconsin stated that the birds had died of blunt-force trauma, but that the trauma that had caused the deaths happened in mid-air flight. The birds were dead well before they hit the ground.

The weather radar that night picked up an echo that meteorologists could not explain. The radar indicated high-level clouds in the area and it also picked up the birds at about 100 feet, but there was something else showing on the radar that night. The spokesman for the National Weather Center in North Little Rock said that a non-weather echo appeared at 1,500 feet well over the birds. It was shaped like a mushroom and had absolutely no movement. When asked what it was, the official said that he did not know, but that he did not feel that it was weather related at all. When asked if weather could cause the blunt-force trauma death of large numbers of birds while in flight, he responded, "Yes." He said that high-level thunder or hail could easily do the damage that was seen on New Year's Eve but that there was not any of that in the area. The stormy weather had cleared out long before the birds fell from the sky.

Invisible Wall

One witness who was interviewed said that the birds appeared to be flying into an invisible wall. He said that they did not appear to be disoriented in the air; they seemed to know exactly where they were going, but that once they had fallen from the sky, they were either dead or appeared to be drunk. The surviving birds walked in circles or staggered back and forth, sometimes falling down and refused to fly. There were very few survivors; most died upon impact. Was it a force field generated by an alien space craft or a secret weapon that the government was trying out?

Just minutes prior to the birds being startled into flight, the witnesses that had seen the birds drop from the sky said that they had seen a bright low-level light in the sky. It had been close to where the birds collided into what they referred to as an invisible wall. The light was there for a very short time before disappearing and the birds started dropping. They thought the light was a spotlight directed on the clouds by one of the townspeople out celebrating New Year's. This is what they thought until the birds started dropping in mid-flight, dead. Then they started to think they had witnessed a UFO.

Dead Fish

A couple of days before all the birds died, another strange event happened in the general area. To the west of Beebe in a twelve-mile stretch of the Arkansas River, 80,000 to 100,000 fish died all at the same time. Fishermen started seeing the fish bob up like corks. First it was a few fish, then they were popping out of the water a far as they could see. Within a couple of hours, the banks of the river were covered with fish. A band of dead fish four-foot wide and twelve-miles long could be seen on both sides of the river.

Some of these fish were gathered and sent to the same independent labs that the birds had been sent to. Again the labs reported that they had no idea what had caused the death of so many fish. No toxins of any kind could be found in the fish carcasses. As far as they could tell, the fish had been healthy and there was no trauma of any kind to the bodies. The deaths of so many birds and fish for no apparent reason have government conspiracy theorists trying to explain what is happening.

HAARP

There is a government funded High Frequency Active Auroral Research Program (HAARP) Station in Alaska that is developing several Ionospheric programs for the good of mankind. That is their story, but government conspiracy theorists know better. They feel like the government is developing a new weapon using harmonics and, of course, as with any weapon, testing is a must. New weapons utilizing harmonics or sound cannot be detected

Two days prior to the massive blackbird deaths, thousands of fish died in the Arkansas River. Fishermen stated that it was just a fish or two at first, then, they could see fish bobbing to the surface everywhere. Within hours, a stretch of twelve miles of riverbank on each side was lined with dead fish. *Photo courtesy of the Arkansas Game and Fish Commission.*

by human senses. When directed at a human target, the result would be much like the death of the birds and fish. One minute the target would be alive and healthy, the next minute the target would simply be dead. The tweaking of harmonics can cause severe internal damage. It has been known to cause earthquakes and alter weather patterns, as well. The civilian watch dogs or government conspiracy theorists feel that this was a test in what the scientists thought was a rural unpopulated part of the state. They believe that they were toying with the storm clouds and the birds were collateral damage. They believe that the fish on the other hand were the target of this new scientific wonder.

The End Times?

Is the end of time upon us? Some people in the beleaguered area around Beebe believe that this is more the case. They say all of the signs are in place for the end of time. In a recent poll of Americans, forty-one percent believe that the end of the world will happen by the year 2050. Because the end of time supposedly coincides with

THE END OF TIME

apocalyptic events, these end-of-time revelers say that we are living in the last days. They need no more proof than a few small cataclysmic events to make them say, "I told you so."

By September of 2010, the area around Beebe has had over 300+ minor earthquakes, each one getting more intense. The most recent earthquake measured a 4.9 on a scale with 10 being the worst. It shook the ground for over a minute and could be felt 150 miles away in the capital city. The area residents grow more and more concerned as these events grow in scale. A few birds and fish dying is normal, but when thousands die within a small, confined area in a short period of time, people start to wonder. Combine the deaths of the fish and the birds with erratic weather patterns and earthquakes, and the same people who started to wonder quietly become scared, volatile panic-driven mobs looking for answers. They are ready to turn on you for offering answers with which they do not agree.

Is the world ending soon? I don't know and I don't know that anybody ever will know. If a person were to believe what the Bible teaches, then it clearly states in 2 Peter 3:10 that the end will come as a thief in the night, and that is probably best for all of mankind.

Beebe is a small farming community northeast of Little Rock. To get to Beebe take US 167/67 north out of Little Rock. It is a short drive of 35 miles. Take Exit 28 and continue east until you see the welcome to Beebe sign.

The Fouke Monster

Fouke, Arkansas

A Monstrous Evening

In May of 1971, a resident of Fouke, Arkansas, Elizabeth Ford, was relaxing on the sofa in her living room when she was suddenly and violently attacked by what can only be described as a monster. As she was lying on the sofa, a hairy, clawed arm burst through the window and tried to grab her. She fought to escape the grip of the creature and eventually wrestled herself free, but she will never forget the red eyes that stared at her as the monster tried to drag her through the window.

Moments later, her husband, Bobby, returned from his hunting trip with his brother. After hearing what had just happened to his wife just minutes before, he and his brother set off with their hunting rifles and flashlights. The men searched the area around the house and saw something moving in the flashlight's beam. The men shot at the creature and saw it fall to the ground. As they headed out to investigate what they had shot, the women, who were still back at the house, began screaming.

Bobby immediately ran toward the house, jumped up onto the front porch, and was attacked by the creature. The monster—which he described as being seven feet tall and ape-like with a chest at least three feet wide—grabbed Bobby by the shoulder and tried to pull him closer. Bobby was able to break free and ran into the house so fast and hard that he did not slow down to open the screen door—he ran straight through it. He and his brother fired into the woods several more times hoping to hit the creature, but no carcass was ever found.

Bobby was injured and suffering from shock; his wife, Elizabeth, knew she had to get him to the hospital fast, but was understandably wary of walking outside to the car. Knowing she had no choice, she grabbed Bobby and dragged him to the car as fast as she could. They sped away to the home of the local Constable, Ernest Walraven. When they arrived, it was obvious to Walraven that Bobby needed medical attention and he took them to the hospital, where Bobby was treated for the deep claw marks and symptoms of shock.

There was no way the Fords were going back to their house that night; instead, they stayed at the home of the Constable. In the morning, they headed back to the house to investigate the scene. It had rained during the night, so any blood evidence or tracks in the forest would have washed away, but they did find some strange tracks on the porch with a small smattering of blood. The Fords had only recently moved into their house and decided there was no way they could ever sleep there again and moved shortly after the attack. They never set foot on the property again.

The site of the last reported sighting of the Fouke Monster. The sighting was by a fisherman, and only for a moment. Feeling as if he was being watched, the fisherman scanned the bank to see if another fisherman had joined him. As he did, he saw a reddish-brown blur in the woods. Once his eyes acclimated, he was able to see a head, arms, and legs as the beast turned to leave. He was not sure what he saw, but knew it was not something he had seen in the woods before or wanted to see again.

Boggy Creek Monster
Fouke, AR

At a small gas station/diner/museum in Fouke, Arkansas, a person may take a picture with the Fouke Monster; and hear the wild stories about personal encounters with the Monster or, as the locals call him, the Boggy Creek Monster.

A Monster Circus

Reports of the Ford's encounter quickly spread beyond the borders of Fouke. Soon reporters, tourists, and Bigfoot hunters alike descended on the small town like locusts. It was a circus-like environment. There were people offering rewards to the person who could capture the monster and bring its dead carcass forth. Dozens of hunters set off into the surrounding swamps and forests to find and kill the famous creature. It got so far out of hand that the local sheriff had to impose a three-day gun ban, for the safety of the public. Around this time, three men were charged with filing false reports of seeing the monster. The men showed up with multiple scratches, but their stories were immediately suspect when one officer noticed the men had dried blood under their fingernails, where they had scratched themselves in order to fake an attack.

In the following weeks, similar sightings were being reported all over the country. People in rural areas were afraid to go outside after dark and worried about the safety of their livestock. Many farmers sat outside at night, watching their animals with a flashlight in one hand and shotgun in the other. As soon as someone reported the creature had been seen, tourists gleefully converged on the area, hoping for just a glimpse. Trespassing turned into a major problem virtually overnight and the throngs of hopeful monster hunters were trampling farmer's crops. After a few months, things began to settle down and life went back to normal for most.

More Attacks

Then in 1977, more sightings were reported. A local farmer went to check on his livestock. What he found was a bloody mess of hogs that had literally been ripped apart. There was blood everywhere; the pigs had not only been killed, they had been mangled. Their stomachs had been ripped open; intestines were littered around the area mixed in with heads and limbs. One pig was found out of the pen several yards away; it was found mutilated, as if something had simply torn it open, and eaten the insides, leaving behind the empty carcass.

In another incident reported in 1977, a man was out hunting for squirrel. The entire time that he had been in the woods, he had felt as if he was being watched. He moved deeper into the woods and felt sure something was following him. He claimed that it would match him step for step and moved in tandem with him as not to give away its location. The man never actually saw the creature, but he could feel it watching him. Eventually, the man fled for his truck, believing that whatever was out there was stalking him and would eventually attack if he did not leave the area. The man has never returned to that part of the woods.

There are more recent reports, as late as 1998 a young woman, out taking a stroll with her nieces and nephews, saw something on the side of the road ahead of the group. As they got closer she saw the shape of a large creature peering out at them. She described the creature as being over six feet tall with dark brownish-colored fur. She stated that it just stood there curiously watching them as they walked toward it. She told the kids they would have to be getting home and quickly turned them around and headed away from the creature, all the while expecting it to jump from the woods and attack at anytime. The creature did not attack and everyone made it home safely, but the woman never forgot how the creature stared at them as they'd walked towards it.

What Is It?

So what exactly is The Fouke Monster? Do we have any proof at all that it exists? Actually, we do have some proof in the form of footprints that were found at one of the sightings. The prints were cast, and what they revealed was the large footprint of a creature that has only three toes. The footprints have been examined many times and most agree that they are the print of a Cryptid. Cryptid is the name given for a creature in the study of cryptozoology which means its existence has been suggested, but not proven to a scientific consensus.

These types of creatures have been sighted for years. The reports are usually very similar: The creature is large, six to seven feet tall with an ape-like appearance. The one thing that gives it away is the horrendous, putrid smell that comes with most sightings. They are almost always sighted around vast wooded areas, which is why some researchers believe they are so hard to capture. They are elusive by necessity and usually only expose themselves to sightings when they are out looking for food, which may be one reason why most sightings are by farmers with livestock.

The sightings have not stopped just because the news coverage has. In 1997, the creature was seen and reported some forty different times. Then in 1998, it was seen again just five miles from Fouke in a dry creek bed. One man even claims to know where the creature calls home. One evening, while out looking for deer, the man came upon what he claims was the most disgusting odor he had ever smelled. The man took off through the woods looking for the source of the foul order and that is when he found the cave, just near the Sulphur River. This is where the man claims the creature's lair is hidden. The site is littered with animal bones and the cave entrance is well hidden. "Unless you were looking for it, you wouldn't know it was there, unless you followed the smell!" the man claimed.

Whether or not The Fouke Monster actually exists is still up for debate. The scientists who have investigated the sightings claim that there is no way such a creature could exist in the Arkansas backwoods. Believers scoff at the idea that scientists know everything there is to know about the swamplands that surround Fouke. One thing, in particular, the scientists point to is that no ape-like creature has only three toes. Even those that are heavily involved in the study of Bigfoot and creatures of this sort remain puzzled by this. Every track ever found that is attributed to some sort of Sasquatch has four or five toes. The Fouke Monster is the only one with just three toes.

This remains a point of contention for many researchers, but if the creatures themselves cannot be explained, how do we explain things like how many toes one might, or might not, have. It seems like a silly argument when talking about a creature who many describe as a monster. No matter what the researchers say, the believers will not back down. They know what they have seen and no scientists from any university will ever change their minds, especially when new species of creatures are being found on an almost-yearly basis.

With dozens of these cryptid sightings every year, it is impossible to dismiss them as merely folklore. The fear that these modern day monsters have spread is real. The bloody carcasses and destroyed property is real. To those who have seen it, the monster is real.

Visit Fouke, Arkansas if you wish to learn more or look for the monster yourself. The locals will tell you the stories, show you the castings of the creature's foot, and maybe even sell you a souvenir or two. If you are lucky, the local theater will be showing the docudrama that was produced about The Fouke Monster in the 1970s. *The Legend of Boggy Creek* will take you through the swamps and backwoods of Fouke, in search of the monster.

The undiscovered mystery lies out there, in those dark, endless swamps and woods. Are you brave enough to go searching for it?

To find The Fouke Monster, start looking to the south of Texarkana in the swamps around the small Miller County community of Fouke. Take I-30 West out of Little Rock. Go about 139 miles and exit at Exit 2 onto AR 245 south. Keep a close watch for AR 549 south to Fouke. Good hunting.

Dr. DEATH

Crescent Hotel
Eureka Springs,
Arkansas

Norman Baker was a self-proclaimed savior of mankind. He had a magical cure for cancer, and was willing to share that cure with people who were prepared to pay his exorbitant fees. He was supposedly a doctor of medicine, but according to many associates, he was actually a rogue and a quack. He promised great things to dying people. He offered them hope, but gave them death. Baker was a kindly-looking man that dressed in a white suit and a lavender tie. He had the mannerisms of a used-car salesman, and seemed to be everybody's best friend. He was, in reality, a self-centered man, who only served his own best interests. Baker referred to the Crescent Hotel as his castle in the air.

Some Historic Background

The Crescent Hotel was built in 1886 as an exclusive getaway for the wealthy. The pleasant surroundings attracted people from all over America. Visitors could enjoy many pursuits designed to make their visit memorable: riding in the morning and enjoying afternoon tea, while making plans to attend a dance in the evening. During its first fifteen years, the Crescent became famous for its southern

The Crescent Hotel is considered the jewel of the Ozarks and the most haunted hotel west of the Mississippi River. Haunted tours are available daily.

hospitality and magnificent architecture. Isaac Taylor was appointed architect by Powell Clayton, former Governor of Arkansas, and his associates. Taylor was instructed to make the Crescent Hotel the most luxurious in America. His design called for Edison lamps for the lighting, electric bells, steam heating, modern indoor plumbing, and a rare hydraulic elevator. The furnishings for all of the rooms were imported, and very expensive. It was a showplace of modern convenience and luxury. The hotel was a huge success, and for several years, America's wealthiest could be found walking the streets of Eureka Springs.

In 1907, the Frisco Railroad took over management of the hotel and the glory days were soon gone. The combination of economic decline and new management resulted in a decline of tourism in Eureka Springs. As a result of the loss of revenue, the railroad closed the hotel and it fell into disrepair. The Crescent was then converted into the Crescent College and Conservatory for Young Women. The school lasted for several years, but due to high overhead, it was forced to close in 1924. Other business ventures were attempted at the Crescent, only to end in failure. The one business that maintained a profitable profile was the hospital and health resort of torture. Norman Baker leased the hotel in 1937 to serve as his own haven for the critically ill. He offered natural healing techniques for cancer, rather than radiation and radical surgeries. His cures sounded so appealing, people came from all over the United States to be healed.

The actual cure Norman Baker offered was mostly exercise and spring water, while he used the unsuspecting patients as guinea pigs for his more invasive experiments. He carved away at the dead as well as the living. As his patients died, he hid the bodies until they could be secretly burned or buried. When a patient entered the hospital, he had them sign several blank letters. After they died, he continued to send letters home to the family enticing them to send more money. This is eventually what led to his undoing. By 1940, he had been arrested and convicted of mail fraud and medical fraud. He was, however, sentenced to only four years in federal prison. The only silver lining to this cloud is that once he had served his time, he disappeared and was never heard from again.

Ghostly Goings On

During remodeling over the years, human skeletons have been found in the walls and buried on the grounds. Since there are no records of any burials on the grounds, the identity of these bodies is unknown.

Michael's Room

During construction of the Crescent Hotel, a worker fell to his death. The location of his demise is believed to be room 218; and this room has become known as "Michael's Room." Over the years, staff and visitors have reported numerous sightings of supernatural apparitions in Room 218. Visitors to Michael's Room have reported the presence of a young white male spirit who is both seen and heard. A salesman staying in Room 218 reported having his shoulder shaken until he was awake, and then hearing someone running away. Others have had doors slammed in their face. One young woman reported the TV coming on and changing channels all night, by itself. Others have told of the water in the bathtub coming on or being turned off by unseen hands.

A Lurking Customer

Another ghost that roams the ornate halls of the hotel is a well-dressed man with a beard and mustache. He tends to hang out in the lobby of the hotel and some staff members have seen him lurking by the old counter at customer check-in. A young bellman approached, what appeared to be, a patron late one night and asked if he might assist him. The elderly patron ignored the young man and continued looking straight ahead, as if he was the only one in the room. It was not until the bellman began following the elderly gentleman that he received a response. The bellman followed him up the stairs, and at the landing between the first and second floors, he stopped, turned and stared at the bellman. Although he did not say a word, the bellman immediately knew he wanted to be left alone. He stood on the landing and watched as the man disappeared.

Basement Recreation Room

There appears to be another ghost in the Basement Recreation Room. At one time, the hotel had an antique switchboard in the lobby as an inoperative centerpiece. One night, the desk clerk was having problems with the old switchboard. The problem was that it worked. The board would light up from time to time, indicating an incoming call from the basement. When the clerk would answer, no one was on the other end of the line. He finally tired of this, believing he was the victim of a practical joke; so, he went to the basement and found the door locked, but saw the phone off the hook. He opened the door, hung up the phone, and went back to work. A few minutes later, the board lit up again, indicating a phone call coming in from the same location. When he went to the basement this time, the phone was not off the hook, and he felt like he was not alone. The old switchboard was removed soon after, and the clerk refused to go back to the basement ever again.

Phantom Nurse

There have been several sightings of a nurse pushing a gurney down the hallway in the middle of the night. It appears that the nurse pushes the gurney down the hall until she comes to a wall, then pushes it through the wall and disappears. I have personally seen this one. I was on one of the haunted tours when I heard something behind me; I turned and witnessed something like a scene from an old movie. The red-headed nurse wore a white uniform with long sleeves that buttoned at the wrist. The dress hung below her knees and she wore a white little stiff hat with a cross in the middle. She was pushing a gurney with what appeared to be a covered body on it. I was distracted and turned away. When I looked back she was gone.

Room 419

In room 419, a ghost known as Miss Theadora will block the door, making it next to impossible to get in or out. One of our investigators stayed in this room and met Miss Theadora. The investigator had been sleeping when something woke her. Miss Theadora said it was *her* room and she wanted my investigator to go down the hall and tell the people in the next room to be quiet. Apparently, whatever they were doing was disturbing Miss Theadora. The investigator spent a good portion of the night trying to explain why she could not do that.

Seeking Ghosts

Spirit Seekers was allowed to conduct an investigation into the claims that have made the Crescent so alluring to the public. The evening had been an interesting one, even before the contact in room 419. We reserved all of the reportedly haunted rooms; and I spent the night in room 218, Michael's Room. While in Michael's Room, we heard a low hissing voice say, "Get out of my room!" While in the first floor conservatory, we were preparing our equipment when I noticed one of the female investigators turn and act as if she were going to hit the person standing behind her. The strange thing was, no one was behind her. When I asked what was going on, she told me that it felt like she had been pinched; she thought it was her husband and had turned to swat him. While in the basement, my wife heard someone whisper in her ear, "Hey Mom!" It is not uncommon for her to be called "Mom" by spirits. She does not understand why they do it, but they often start a conversation by calling her Mom.

One final encounter, before we all called it a night, was in the Grand Dining Room. One of the investigators had been to the Crescent as a child, and had seen the spirits of a man and woman dancing in the dining room. It had frightened her so much that she could not tell her parents what she was seeing. Now, even though it had been many years since she had seen the dancing couple, she was still afraid to go back in the dining room. But she overcame her fear and covered the room for us. When she entered the room she heard someone say, "Welcome back."

This picture, taken from the balcony of Room 208, is of an energy orb hovering above the railing as if to say, "Welcome to my room." It is called Michael's Room because, during construction, a young worker named Michael fell to his death, and Room 208 is where his body landed. The room is considered to be very haunted.

We had many personal experiences at the Crescent during our investigation; and recorded one exceptional piece of evidence. Remember the female investigator who felt as if she had been pinched while standing in the Conservatory? She stayed in the Conservatory that night despite the fact that the contact had scared her.

She took lots of pictures and one of them turned out to be extraordinary; the type of evidence that paranormal investigators wait a lifetime to get. This outstanding photograph was of a female apparition standing half-in and half-out of the room. The photograph was so detailed that the staff believed they could identify the woman. They had an old picture of the teaching staff while the Crescent was a school for women, and one of the women in the photograph looked just like the ghostly apparition. That photograph was so clear that the Crescent Hotel awarded it the Ghost Photograph of the Year in 2005.

The Crescent Hotel in Eureka Springs is one of Arkansas's most haunted places to visit. It is considered by many to be the most haunted hotel west of the Mississippi River.

To get to the good Doctor's castle in the air take I-40 west out of Little Rock to Conway. At Exit 125, head north on US 65. Stay on this highway for about 125 miles, then merge onto US 62 west and stay on this road until you get to Eureka Springs. While you are at the Crescent Hotel, say hi to Michael for us.

Hang'em High and Often

*Judge Parker T's
Court and Gallows
Fort Smith, Arkansas*

The fabled courthouse where Hanging Judge Parker ruled his territory with an iron fist. It is located in Fort Smith, Arkansas, and is operated as a museum by the National Park Service.

The six men stood perfectly still on the wooden-planked floor. It was a hot day in the Fort Smith territory. The men's hands were secured behind their backs while the wind blew dust across their boots. The six men stared out at the crowd that had gathered to watch their demise. They were murderers and rapists, the worst kind of men to be, especially in this territory. The ropes were placed around their necks while a preacher prayed for their souls. Without warning, the hatch in the floor gave way and the six men dropped to their deaths. They hung there, some still twitching from the broken neck issued by the hangman's noose. This is what happened to men when they broke the law in the "Hanging Judge's" territory.

Some Hanging History

From 1875-1896, Judge Isaac Charles Parker was the federally appointed judge for the Fort Smith territory. His area of responsibility stretched far across the western half of Arkansas and into Oklahoma, and included many Indian tribal nations as well. Parker was dubbed the "Hanging Judge." During his time on the bench, he presided over 12,000 criminal cases. Of the men who had their day in his court, 160 were sentenced to die at the end of a rope. Of those, only 79 eventually ended up with the noose around their necks. Nevertheless, that is a great many souls to have on one man's conscious. What many people are not aware of is that Judge Parker was actually against the death penalty. He argued that it was not a deterrent to crime, but his hands were tied. In those days, the law said there was only one punishment for murder and rape. That punishment was death.

Parker's guilt over ordering the death of so many men may be one reason he still haunts his own gallows. The original gallows and a replica of the courthouse are now a national park and thousands of visitors wander around the area where men were executed with such fervor. Many visitors report odd feelings when standing on the gallows. It is not entirely the uneasiness of standing where so many condemned souls once stood—it is something different, something supernatural.

Court Still in Session

A former employee tells of a particularly frightful experience she had one night while working late. She had gone into the replica of Parker's courtroom to make sure all the visitors were gone. When she went to shut off the light, she heard what could only be a gavel being struck against Judge Parker's bench. She looked around trying to find another source for the noise, but found none. She shrugged it off, and as she turned to leave, she heard voices behind her. The voices were those of angry men. They were shouting and she could hear the gavel being slammed down again. The voices became louder until they were all around her. She spun in every direction looking for anyone that may be there. Then she started to see a heavy mist envelope the courtroom. The mist was over the defendant's table, but it quickly spread around the room and

Inside the courtroom where hundreds of men and women were sentenced to die at the end of a rope. The Judge has been seen by staff and visitors sitting at his desk as if waiting for the next case. The sound of a pounding gavel has been heard slamming down on the desk, demanding order in his court.

was soon at the prosecutors table; all the while the voices raged on. Men were yelling and she could hear a woman crying.

She stood there, too petrified to move, as the scene played out in front of her. The mist was becoming heavier and was soon covering the entire front of the courtroom. She heard footsteps coming up behind her and she turned to see the partial apparition of a man in dusty clothes with grime covering his face being dragged away by two other men wearing badges. The scene was fading in and out like a television with bad reception. The voices were calmer now, more like murmuring than shouting. She heard the Judge's gavel strike once more and then all went quiet. The voices stopped and the mist began to fade away. She stood there dumbstruck for a few minutes while she tried, and failed, to make sense out of what she had just experienced.

Fort Smith National Cemetery

Personal experiences are the norm when it comes to Judge Parker's courtroom, and especially the surrounding area. Not far from the gallows is the Fort Smith National Cemetery where Judge Parker and his wife are buried. The graveyard also holds the corpses of many of those he ordered hanged, along with several of his marshals. The cemetery is a beautiful place that holds the history of a once-wild west in its hallowed grounds. However, some say the ground does not hold everyone who was buried there. Some get away.

On a cold December, night in 1998 a groundskeeper had an experience that left him shaken to the core. The worker, we will call Steve, had left some tools in one of the sheds on the grounds. The night was quickly enveloping the graves as Steve headed out to retrieve his tools. The dead, frozen grass crunched under his work boots as he made his way and he thought he heard something behind him. So he stopped and turned around. Steve was not the nervous type. He had worked in graveyards for years and had long ago gotten over the creepiness of it, that still makes most of us cringe at the thought of being in a cemetery after dark.

When he turned to investigate the noise, he did not see anything so he continued on his way. Again, he heard something; he slowed his stride so he could pinpoint its location, without turning around. The sound was getting closer and louder. The closer it got to him, the more familiar it got. It was almost on top of him when he realized it was footsteps that he was hearing. Steve swung around to confront whoever was following him...and still no one was there. He hurried to the shed and retrieved his tools and grabbed a flashlight before heading back.

Switching on the flashlight, Steve started walking. He had made it maybe ten feet when he again heard the crunch of footsteps behind him. He swung around again, and in the beam of his flashlight, there was an old man. The man stood there looking back at him. Steve looked closely at the man and realized he could see *through* him. The apparition was still standing there looking distinguished with white hair and a white beard, dressed in an old black suit.

Steve asked the man what he wanted, but he only stared back at him. Steve then warned him that he was going to call the police, and if this was some kind of joke, he should leave immediately. Then the man pointed at him and started moving his mouth as if he were talking to Steve, but no sound came from his lips. The empty eyes of the apparition widened and his mouthing motions became more animated. Steve realized he was in a situation he could not control and fear began to take hold of him. He turned away from the man and began to run. As he looked over his shoulder, he could see the ghostly trespasser and that he was still pointing. Steve dropped his flashlight, and not wanting to waste time stopping for it, he just ran as fast as he could.

When Steve got to his car, he stopped and turned around again. The apparition was gone. Steve has many questions about that night. First, what did the spirit want and why was he pointing at him? Steve knew who the spirit was. He had been to the museum and he'd seen the photos of Judge Parker—and there is no doubt in his mind that this was whose ghost he saw that night. The "why" still bothers him. The Judge's face mouthing words with no sound still haunts his nightmares. He left the employ of the park soon after this incident.

Steve no longer works in cemeteries and never will again.

The Gallows

The infamous gallows are another location that has frequent paranormal activity surrounding it. One tourist was witness to this and is forever changed because of it. Jessica was born and raised in Fort Smith and knew all about Judge Parker's gallows. She had heard stories about the "Hanging Judge" ever since she was a little girl. She and some of her friends from out of town decided to visit the park. She had been there many times, but her friends had never been, and wanted to see the gallows before they went home. Being the agreeable host, Jessica and her friends prepared for a day at the museum.

Jessica's friends were more impressed with the museum and the replica of the courtroom than they were with the gallows. While they looked around inside, Jessica wandered outside to get some air and look at the gallows. It was

The recreated gallows where Parker's final judgments were carried out. Notice the bright orb hanging over the gallows. Visitors have reported seeing hanging men as they walked through the site.

a normal day at the park. People were walking around, many of them snapping photos of the gallows, and making jokes. Jessica found some tourists' comments completely inappropriate, and their jokes unfunny. To Jessica, this was sacred ground. People had died there, sure—they were criminals—but they had paid the price for their crimes with their lives and did not deserve the disrespectful comments.

She stood watching the people mill around for a while. When she looked back up at the gallows, she lost her breath. In the middle of the hanging beam on the gallows, a man was there. He appeared to be in his thirties, wearing dirty clothes and worn-out boots. Around his neck was the rope and he was hanging from it. The man was obviously dead, and at first, Jessica thought it might be an actor; maybe they were doing a reenactment. Surely, she thought, they would not have such a gruesome display for a reenactment in a place where there were children running around daily.

She stared at the man as he swayed in the air for a long minute and she realized that no one else was looking at him. They could not see him; only she could see the ghostly image of death that was before her. As she stared, holding her breath without realizing it, she watched as tourist after tourist walked right through the man, never realizing they were touching a ghost.

Suddenly, the man's eyes opened and he was staring directly at her, his head tilted at a grotesque angle where the noose had snapped his neck. The long dead outlaw just stared at her and then grinned showing his blackened teeth. Jessica turned away horrified; when she gained enough courage to look again, the apparition was gone.

There is little doubt, if any, that Judge Parker and the men he had hanged still wander the area. The death and anguish that took place there left an undeniable scar on the landscape of time. If you are brave enough to visit, be sure and obey the law. The local judges are known to be quite strict.

To get to Judge Parkers Court and Gallows, head west young man, head west. Take I-40 west out of Little Rock and stay the course for about 150 miles. You should arrive at your destination in roughly two and a half hours. Judge Parker's Court and Gallows is located at Third and Garland Streets.

Sheriff Ike

1872 Hempstead County Jail
Washington, Arkansas

The city of Washington, Arkansas, is one of the state's oldest cities. It was incorporated in 1824, well before Arkansas became a state.

As the city began to decline in the 1870s, a new county courthouse and a new county jail were planned and constructed to help bolster the city's economy and preserve its place as the county seat. The new two-story jail was built in 1872, and in 1874, a new two-story brick courthouse was built. They both served the Hempstead County until 1939, when the county seat was transferred to Hope and a new courthouse and jail was built.

The Old Washington Jail Bed and Breakfast Inn is a beautiful old two-story building situated about two blocks from the 1874 Courthouse. The building looks more like an antebellum mansion built for local aristocrats than a county jailhouse. The dining room still has "graffiti" from the original occupants. The walls and ceilings are made of two-foot-thick concrete which makes an already tranquil setting more serene.

Many of the guests have commented that their stay was very peaceful, but that is not all that guests have said about the old jailhouse.

The old jail was abandoned in 1939 and sat for a very long time unattended. The place was converted into a boarding house in the '40s and remained such until 1980 when it was converted into a bed and breakfast. Today, the Washington Jail Bed and Breakfast is privately owned. The owners have restored the old jail to its original splendor, with some minor changes. Visitors and guests are no longer locked behind bars and made to sleep on hard, lumpy beds, but rather a person is treated to luxurious accommodations. They are no longer escorted to their rooms by burly men carrying guns and handcuffs; they are met at the door with a friendly smile and a big Arkansas welcome. Oh yes, one other thing, they are also met at the door by the resident Ghost.

The Sheriff of Nevada County, Arkansas, was incarcerated and held for trial in the Hempstead County Jail in 1920. The Hempstead County Jail is now known as the Old Washington Jail Bed and Breakfast Inn. Nevada County is a neighboring county to the south. The sheriff was held in the Hempstead County Jail mainly because he was arrested in Hempstead County, but also because it was felt that the he would either be lynched by the local women of Nevada County or set free by his deputies.

Good Gone Bad

It appears that the sheriff had a good life in Nevada County. He was obviously popular because he was elected to office. He had a good wife and good children. But as is the case with some people, the sheriff began to want more out of life. He felt that he was not getting the attention from his wife that he deserved, so

The Old Hempstead County Jail. It is located in the city of Washington, Arkansas.

This column is covered with names of inmates that served time in the old jail. It is located in the common room where prisoners were allowed a few minutes out of their cell each day.

he turned his attention to his stepdaughter. In the '20s, an extra marital affair was absolutely shameful, but an affair with your stepdaughter was unallowable. The girl got pregnant and nature began to reveal the dark secret she'd withheld from her mother. When the sheriff's wife, the daughter's mother, found out what had been going on behind her back, she was furious. She confronted the sheriff and a fight followed. Mother and daughter left Ike soon after she had confronted him.

While waiting on a train in Hope, Arkansas, Mother and daughter were approached by Ike, the Sheriff. He did everything he could to stop them from leaving, to no avail. When all else failed, the sheriff drew his gun to stop them from boarding the train. By then, the Hope Police and the county sheriff had been summoned to the train station to stop what appeared to be a killing in progress. The sheriff was arrested and hauled off to the Hempstead County lock up to await trial. His sinful ways had caught up with him.

While locked up in the Old Washington Jail (Hempstead County Jail), he had time to think about his crime. He decided that he was a branded man and had little or no hope of a future if released from jail. He feared for his life. Rather than face the ridicule and hopelessness of a failed life, he made a decision to hang himself. One evening after the final cell check, he took his bed sheet, formed a noose, and executed the justice he felt he deserved. This was particularly difficult in that there was no furniture from which to jump. He literally choked himself to death. The next morning, the Hempstead County Deputy Sheriff found his lifeless body hanging in the cell.

The Sheriff of Nevada County, Ike, as he has become known, remains in the jailhouse serving a self-imposed sentence of eternity in jail.

The owners have reported that he does little things to let them know that he is still around. Some of the guests have been so frightened by things that they have seen that they have left in the middle of the night. The sheriff has been seen walking the halls opening and closing doors as if to check on the residence. He never intends to frighten, but it can be unnerving to have a ghost moving about the house. The sheriff likes to move things and even hide them from unsuspecting visitors. The owner recalls one evening in particular. He had decided to go to bed early and read. The book that he had been reading was left on the bed stand by the bed when he'd retired. The next morning the book was gone. Later the next day, he found the book in his car parked in the drive outside the house.

An Investigation

Because of the stories that are being told about this old jail, it was decided to send a paranormal investigative team to determine if the stories had any merit. Team One of Spirit Seekers was sent to the city of Washington, Arkansas. We all met at the Bed and Breakfast around 9 o'clock in the evening. We each had a room, and after getting settled in, we prepared for a long night. The night started slow, but ended with a bang.

Our team psychic, Rose, began the investigation by walking around inside the house in an effort to determine if and where there was spirit activity. In the Pilkington Room, Rose felt as if she was not alone. Someone or something was

An investigative photo. At the end of the hall, the transparent form of what looks like a man hanging can be seen. Sheriff Ike did hang himself in the same general area of the jail. *Photo courtesy of Spirit Seekers Paranormal Investigation Research and Intervention Team (SPIRIT).*

there with her watching her every move. In the Deloney Room, she felt like something very emotional had happened there. She thought maybe there was a residual haunting. (A residual haunting is like an imprint on time, or a loop where a specific event repeats over and over.) In the Monroe Room, she hit pay dirt. In this room she met Robert. He was a prisoner who had been convicted but swears he did not do it. (While doing an investigation at the old Courthouse, just two blocks away, we encountered a spirit by the name of Robert at that location as well. These two buildings are very close together. This spirit and the other spirit in the courthouse are apparently the same Robert.) While the Psychic was communicating with Robert, I saw what appeared to be a shadow of a person standing close to her. There was very little light in the room, but what I saw was a much darker shape on an already dark wall.

The remainder of the investigation centered on the Monroe Room. While in the house, most of the paranormal data was collected in this room or close by. However, we did manage to gather data throughout the entire house. While there, we collected photographs of spirit energy at rest and in motion. In one picture of the hallway, in which the one-time sheriff is said to have been seen, we can clearly see the apparition of a hanging man. Remember, Sheriff Ike hung himself rather than face justice. After the equipment was put away and the investigators had retired for the evening, the spirit activity increased.

Rose, our team psychic, wanted to stay in the Monroe Room and continue to try to communicate with whatever spirits were there. While in the room, she contended that she was not alone. Rose could feel that the spirit was there, but did not want to communicate and this feeling continued all night. I stayed in the Deloney Room. While there, I slept soundly enough, but was awakened several times by what felt like fingers on my face, neck, and arm. The feeling was aggravating, but not threatening in any way. I also had a headache all night while in the room.

Teri, one of our trainees, stayed in the Pilkington Room. While in this room, she had her eye glasses taken from her face. Although this did frighten her, she said she did not feel threatened. But because she had been frightened, she went out on the front porch to get some air. While out on the front porch, one of the three rocking chairs started rocking as if she had been followed and someone had taken a seat to wait on her return. This was too much for her and she decided to leave and take a room in Hope, Arkansas.

After reviewing the data gathered and listening to the accounts of the investigators, we have concluded that the stories concerning the Old Washington Jail Bed and Breakfast do have merit. All of the spirit activity appears to be benign in nature, and from all accounts received, Ike made an appearance in the Pilkington Room while Robert stayed put in the Monroe Room.

So, when you visit the Old Washington Jail Bed and Breakfast and you see the sheriff walking the halls checking the doors, don't be frightened. He is only doing his job by checking on the visitors and guests to make sure that all is well.

Old Washington Jail Bed and Breakfast can be found in the small city of Washington in the southwest part of the state. To get to Washington, Arkansas, take I-30 west out of Little Rock to Exit 30 and go north on AR 278. Go about 12 miles and there it is. Don't sneeze or you might miss it

An Angry Man

The Powhatan Courthouse
Powhatan, Arkansas

The Powhatan Courthouse sits atop a hill overlooking the city and the Black River.

Standing on a hill overlooking the county it once served, the Powhatan Courthouse is a majestic building. Originally built in 1873, this marvel of Victorian Architecture burned to the ground and had to be completely restored in 1885. The building now houses a museum and is a popular tourist attraction; it is one of the most popular attractions in the area for those who love to visit our state parks. On site are also the original jail and the Flicken-Imboden House. It is easy for one to think they have taken a step back in time when visiting The Powhatan Historic State Park. However, what the tourist brochures will not tell you is that there is something otherworldly going on at this place, something darker and more sinister than just a friendly day at the park.

Investigations

In 2006, Spirit Seekers Paranormal Investigation and Research Team conducted the first of several paranormal investigations of the site. What we found keeps us going back yearly.

The first investigation started around 8 p.m. The beginning order of business was to send in the team psychics to see if they could pinpoint any particular areas where the group should concentrate its efforts. The first psychic that we sent out immediately came upon the spirit of a young, black male playing in the courtroom. The spirit told the psychic that he was sad because he had been murdered and that he stayed at the courthouse because that is where the man who killed him went on trial. The child-spirit soon broke off contact with the psychic and was not seen again that night.

The entire night was incredibly active; investigators were reporting unseen hands grabbing them the way a child trying to get an adult's attention would do. Muffled noises were heard in almost every part of the building; when an investigator would go to investigate, the sounds would stop, and no source could be found. Photographic evidence from the investigation shows what appears to be several spirit orbs floating in and around the sites where these phenomena were reported.

Ghosts in the Belfry

The most terrifying moment of the night happened in the belfry of the courthouse. A female investigator had climbed up narrow, rickety stairs to conduct an EVP (electronic voice phenomena) session. This is a process where the investigator will ask random questions of the spirit in hope of receiving a response. The investigator uses an electronic voice recorder when asking the questions and later plays it back to listen for any responses that could not be heard by the human ear.

Our investigator, who we will call Jan, was asking questions when she was suddenly attacked by an unknown entity. She began to have trouble breathing and could feel her throat tighten, as if an invisible hand were closing around her windpipe. At the same time she was having the breathing problems, she was overcome with feelings of sadness and heaviness in her chest like an enormous amount of grief had been suddenly cast upon her. Jan immediately made her way out of the belfry and back down to the courtroom. After immediately leaving the stairwell that lead to the belfry, the feelings started to subside and her breathing returned to normal. Later, she found a small bruise on her neck as if invisible hands had been attempting to choke the life out of her.

Footsteps and a Scream

At around two in the morning, most of the investigators left for the night. A small team agreed to stay the night and report on what, if anything, happened. Soon after the majority of the team left, the remaining members heard what could only be described as heavy footsteps on one of the staircases. When the investigators arrived at the foot of the staircase, the sound stopped. They stood in the darkness, waiting to hear the sound again. Minutes went by as they waited; they were about to give up and go back to the main courtroom when the footsteps started again. They lasted between five and six seconds then stopped. What happened next is something two of our investigators will never forget. After the footsteps stopped, they started again, only two steps were heard, and then suddenly the high-pitched scream of a woman echoed off the walls. The two investigators stared up towards the top of the staircase in amazement before composing themselves and climbing up the stairs to investigate the source of the scream. They found nothing; no one that could have made the heavy footsteps heard, and no one that could have issued such a blood-curdling scream.

Dowsing for Ghosts

Our second investigation was in May, 2006. We returned in hopes of having more experiences like those we encountered on our first one. We would not be disappointed. The night started out slow; not much was happening as we conducted various experiments and attempted to record EVPs. We decided to use our dowsing rods. Dowsing or divining rods, as some people call them, have been used for

This is an investigative photo taken in the courtroom. The orb appeared while Alan was working with dowsing rods and supposedly communicating with an angry spirit named Andrew. Photo courtesy of Spirit Seekers Paranormal Investigation Research and Intervention Team (SPIRIT).

centuries for everything from finding water underground and lost items to communicating with the dead. We do not know for sure how they work, but there is plenty of circumstantial evidence that they do. When a spirit is encountered, since they are only energy beings at this point, they will use the energy of the dowser to move the rods. We use a simple baseline to establish contact. We ask the spirit to cross the rods if the answer to a question is "yes" or to leave the rods untouched if the answer is "no."

The first contact we made with the rods was that of a black, female spirit who refused to leave the courthouse until her brother, who also haunted the location, moved on. We later found out there was a young black man who had been lynched not far from the courthouse for the crime of rape. The man's name was Andrew Springer, a freed slave who worked as a sharecropper after the Civil War. He was arrested and transported from his native Sharp County to Powhatan in hopes of bringing him to trial and keeping him out of the hands of vigilantes. Andrew never made it to trial. He was abducted somewhere along the way and lynched from an oak tree not far from the courthouse, all the while maintaining his innocence. The great oak where Andrew took his last breath still stands today.

The spirit we were in contact with, who claimed to be Andrew's sister, also died in the area, just 100 yards away in the jail. She was obsessed with clearing her brother's name. After he was lynched, she attempted to exact revenge upon those she felt had caused her brother's death. She was subsequently arrested and placed in jail to await trial where she died of an unknown illness.

After the female spirit broke off contact, Alan and I decided to try and contact Andrew using the dowsing rods. Our team psychic felt strongly that he resided in the

An infrared photo taken in the adjoining jail. A woman died in the jail and is reported to be the sister of the lynched prisoner, Andrew. This streaking orb could be the spirit of the long-dead sister. *Photo courtesy of Spirit Seekers Paranormal Investigation Research and Intervention Team (SPIRIT).*

belfry, which would explain the attack on our female investigator the previous year, so we headed up the staircase and into the belfry, not knowing what to expect.

We decided we would each use a set of dowsing rods so we could gauge whether or not Andrew was strong enough to move them both simultaneously. He was. As we asked our questions it became clear that Andrew did not approve of us being in the courthouse. He also admitted to being the one who attacked Jan the previous year. Andrew continually expressed his hatred for women. It was a woman after all, who according to him, had falsely accused him of rape, thus putting the hangman's noose around his neck.

Andrew's main goal now is to inflict as much discomfort and instill as much fear as he can into anyone he encounters, especially women. Andrew did not make it easy on us while we were questioning him. The air became extremely dry and the temperature seemed to have risen by several degrees. We were both dripping with sweat and we were starting to feel the drain of energy as Andrew answered our questions by moving both sets of rods simultaneously. He was using our energy to move them, and as the questioning dragged on, we finally had to call it quits. We were exhausted and Alan felt as if "something was crawling all over him." It was an obvious sign that Andrew was not a friend and we needed to leave the area before someone got hurt. Alan later told me that he felt as if there were hundreds of fire ants crawling all over him, furiously biting as they moved around his body. When we left the belfry, the pain immediately ceased.

Camera Shots

Later in the evening, an infrared video camera was set up in the jail. The jail is another spot where Andrew's sister had made contact with investigators earlier in the evening. After focusing the camera on one of the iron jail cells, an investigator immediately noticed something coming towards the camera at a high rate of speed. After rewinding the tape and slowing it down, a bright, white light is seen coming straight for the camera, but at the last second changes direction and flies behind it. This happened at about the same time an EVP recording was captured. Could this be the spirit of Andrew's sister? It seems likely that she would attempt to make herself known one last time in the place where her life ended so tragically.

Summation

There is no way for us to verify all the events that transpired which eventually lead to the lynching of Andrew Springer. What we do know is that he was hanged for a crime against a woman. We will never know if Andrew Springer was guilty of that crime for which he was eventually executed. What we do know is that blacks were not treated particularly well after the war ended, and it is not too far of a stretch to believe that Andrew was accused simply because of his race, the only proof of his crime being the accusation of a white person.

So is the Powhatan Historic Park haunted? I believe it is. Along with our encounter with Andrew and his sister, several investigators had experiences of their own that could not be explained.

One investigator was contacted, through dowsing rods, at the Flicken-Imboden House that sits adjacent to the courthouse. In the bedroom on the second floor, the spirit told the investigator that she had died in that very room during childbirth. This story is particularly heartbreaking because the spirit also told the investigator that prior to her death she had lost several children while giving birth in that very room, finally giving her life for the one that lived.

The Powhatan Courthouse is out in the boondocks, but it is a fun day trip. To get there, take US 67/167 north out of Little Rock for about 87 miles to Exit 85. Take Exit 85 or AR-18 toward Newport for about a mile, then turn right on AR-367. That should get you to the old courthouse and jail. It is a very well kept state park with places to picnic and lots to see. If you happen to run into Andrew tell him that we said hi.

The Devil's Hole

Self, Arkansas

There are many gates to Hell in our world and they all have to have a gate keeper. The gate keeper is there not to keep people out, but to keep lost spirits in. One such gate exists in Northwest Arkansas near a little community named Self. This is not a story that many people have heard, but those who have heard the tale of the mighty Gowrow Monster will swear that it is real.

The Mighty Gowrow

The Gowrow gets its name from the sound it makes while devouring its prey. It is said to feast on deer, goats, small cows, horses, and other small woodland creatures. There are those who feel that it would not hesitate eating a human or two given the chance. *Fierce looking* is how it was described by the mountain folk who saw it. It looked like a giant lizard with scaly skin. It was somewhere in the neighborhood of twenty feet in length and had long fangs that looked like tusks. A row of jagged bones ran down its back. The Gowrow's feet were webbed and had claws like a cat.

An artist interpretation of all available descriptions and drawings combined to show what the Gowrow Monster may have looked like. *Rendering courtesy of Violet Renee.*

Native American legend says that the Gowrow is the gate keeper of Hell. Although Native Americans have talked about lizard-like monsters living in caves in the Ozark Mountains, the first recorded contact was close to Blanco, Arkansas, and it is here where our story begins.

On With the Chase!

In the late 1800s, Blanco was a small thriving farming community. A couple of hundred people gathered in one spot trying to eke out a living. They all came from different walks of life, but they all had one very special thing in common: They were afraid to go out after sundown. They had all heard the stories of the Gowrow and some had even seen the monster in action.

In 1897, William Miller, a traveling salesman, was in the area. Blanco, Arkansas, which was a small community in Searcy County. Miller had been going from house to house listening to the stories of the great and fierce Gowrow monster. His interest in the animal was high when he made his last stop of the day in Blanco. The family at this house told him that as recently as the night before the Gowrow had paid them a visit. The owner of the property had gone out to get some eggs for breakfast and walked in the barn during the final stages of a feeding frenzy. The monster was startled by his appearance and ran out the back of the barn through a hole that it had made coming in.

William Miller asked to be shown this hole in the barn. When he entered, he saw for himself the slaughter from the previous nights feeding of the Gowrow and then the hole from which the great monster made good its escape. Fortunately for Miller, it had snowed the night before and the creature had left tracks leading away into the woods. The next morning Miller organized a posse to hunt down the dangerous beast. The help he expected from the locals was not in abundance in that most of the men had seen what the Gowrow could do when cornered. Even at that, a few of the community men volunteered to go along. They tracked the animal to the river where they lost it tracks. Evidently, the Gowrow could swim.

It was here that they split up and followed the river until one group found tracks coming out and heading back into the woods. Once the separated group had joined forces again, they began to follow the newly found tracks. The trail of the Gowrow was followed until they disappeared into a very large cave. The cave was deep and dark, so Miller found the makings of a torch and entered the cave. He found the cave to be empty except for the bones of eaten animals.

After a lengthy conversation, the posse decided to wait outside for the return of the beast. They lay a trap for the returning animal. All of the men were armed with shotguns and rifles. When the monster returned the men took aim and fired their weapons. The Gowrow shook as if being tickled, so they fired again and again until it lay dying in the mouth of the cave. Once the great beast was dead, Miller approached it to assure that it would never bother the good people of Blanco again.

This story appeared in the *Arkansas Gazette* and is considered to be a good campfire story and nothing else. If that is true, how do we explain other sightings in the same general area?

A Bottomless Pit

Self, Arkansas is located approximately eight miles north of Harrison in Boone County. Self is not too far to the east and south of Blanco. An exact date of when the first family settled in the area is unknown, but it is thought that it was in the late 1800s, just like Blanco. The difference between the two is that the Self community grew due, in large part, to the railroad that came through the area. It became a stopover for the railway where livestock was loaded for the market. Buildings were built to provide cover for services that supported the train and cattle industry. A post office was established in 1906 making Self a federally recognized community that is still active today.

The second noted report comes from the area around Self. A local farmer named E. J. Rhodes owned some property on which a giant cavern could be found. The mouth of the cave opened into the side of Flint Hill, then dropped sharply down into a bottomless pit. This bottomless pit became known as the Devil's Hole.

All that is known about Rhodes' involvement with the Devil's Hole is that he descended down on a rope to about 300 feet. At that point, he became frightened and signaled to be pulled out. He said that he got worried about earth gasses that far down and decided that it would be best to not go any further down. The truth be known, he had heard what sounded like a deep throat growl that made him want to get out of the hole.

Some years later a man named Jim Summers went to the cavern to try to make soundings to determine the depth. He had taken a thousand feet of clothesline rope thinking that should be plenty. A heavy iron was attached to one end of the rope and thrown in. The iron stopped at about 200 feet each time an attempt was made. It was known that a ledge existed in that area because the first man to explore it had mentioned that he had paused on a ledge at 200 feet to rest before going on. On this day, the rope was not going past the 200-foot depth.

Before trying again, strange tracks were seen in the dirt around the hole. It was known that many animals had gone into the cave and never returned, but these tracks were like no animal Jim had ever seen. One more toss of the iron into the hole got Jim nowhere. The iron stopped in the same place every time.

One thing different *this* time was that a vicious growl or hiss could be heard from the depths of the hole. When the flatiron was retrieved, it had been bent.

Upon examination of the iron, it was noted to have, what looked like, teeth marks on it. This made Summers wonder what might be down there, so he removed the iron and tied a rock on the line instead. When he cast the line in this time, it landed in much the same place, only it made a different sound. It sounded more cushioned, like it had hit something soft. When he drew the line back, the rock was gone and the line looked as if it had been cut. Three more attempts netted the same results; each time before bringing the line up, a hiss could be heard from the depths of Devil's Hole.

Is this just another fine story invented by a reporter to sell newspaper copy. Maybe, but then there are many facts contained in the story that can be verified. The hole is there, the names of the participants are factual, and the mysterious stories of the Gowrow continue to come out of the Ozarks.

Tall Tales?

A writer by the name of Vance Randolph not only wrote about the monster, but claims to have seen it personally. Vance Randolph was known for his tall tales and published a book titled *We Always Lie to Strangers*. In this book, written in 1951, Randolph wrote about a man in Mena, Arkansas who claimed to have captured a Gowrow Monster. Mena is a little to the south and west of the other two sightings, but still in the Ozarks Mountain Range. This man claimed to have laid a trap for the monster with apples. Once he had him caged, he charged admission to see the monster. Strange thing was that every time he took a group back to see it, all they saw was a torn-up cage. He then got all excited and claimed that it must be on the loose and yelled for everyone to run for their lives.

Is this a tall tale told by a very good writer? Probably. Is this a tale of a man trying to dupe the public out of some hard-earned cash? Maybe. Does this mean that the story of the Gowrow Monster is not true? Not necessarily. The story of the monster has survived through Native American mythology and Anglo American lore to be told repeatedly through the generations. The monster has been reported in the mountains of Missouri, Oklahoma, and Arkansas by hundreds of people.

The latest report of the fabled Gowrow came to me while doing research for this story. A local resident close to Jasper near the Buffalo River told me that every once in awhile he can hear a wailing noise drifting through the mountains that makes his skin crawl. When I asked what he thought it was, he said that he didn't know but that it sounded like a monster.

Skeptics will tell you that it was probably just the wind blowing through the trees. Or, it could have been a bull elk looking for love. Then again, there are those who will swear to you that it sounded just like the Gowrow devouring a meal.

The trip to Self, Arkansas is a long one, but well worth the time. When you leave Little Rock, take I-40 west to Conway. At Conway, take Exit 125 and turn right onto US 65 north for about 115 miles. The Devil's Hole is close, but you may have to ask someone exactly where it is at this point. Watch your step; the Gowrow is close.

Chosen

Searcy, Arkansas

Searcy is a city located about an hour north of Little Rock; it is a small, quiet community. It is generally not thought of as a tourist attraction, although I am sure some would disagree. One person in particular would be a local resident who we will call Lisa. Lisa would tell you that Searcy is of interest to a special group of tourists. Tourists who need no passport, and are not interested in the local sites. This special group of visitors arrives, for the most part, unseen by the population at large. They arrive in the darkness and bring with them unimaginable terror.

The story begins in October, 2007; it is a favorite time for Arkansans. The summer heat is finally fading, and people are getting ready for Halloween. Lisa too looked forward to this time of year; she was just like everyone else. Which is why she still asks to this day, "Why me?" She has no special talents or medical conditions that make her unique. There are no earthly reasons for her to be chosen out of thousands of potential victims. However, that is what she was: chosen.

It was a normal day for Lisa; she was on her way home from work when she stopped by the local store to pick up some things. A friend had called and asked if she would stop by for a bit and hang out for some girl talk and a glass of red wine. Excited at the prospect of having some company for the evening, Lisa set off towards her friend's house. Lisa never arrived.

She remembers very little about the initial abduction, where she was taken from her car. She remembers an intense feeling of heat and a "sort of pulling at my chest." She stated that "there was a bright light, surrounded by dozens of smaller, colored lights, all of which were blinking in different patterns." What happened next is a nightmare she will never be able to forget.

> I woke up in a small, dark room. The first thing I remember thinking is that it was very cold and wishing that I had a blanket. I was on a long table, maybe ten feet long and four feet wide. I realized I was naked when the coldness of the table began to sting against my back. When I tried to get up, I couldn't move. I was being held down by something, but I couldn't see anything that might have been restraining me. I could lift my head up off the table, but that's as far as I could go. Even that was difficult; it felt as if my head weighed fifty pounds.

Lisa described the room she was kept in as eggshell white, like a type of porcelain, but not porcelain. After lying on the table for what seemed like hours, she began to hear a murmur of voices. Only the voices were not speaking aloud; they were inside of her head. It sounded like a dozen different people all talking at once. She could not make out anything that was being said; every time a voice would start to speak another one would start talking over the first one. The voices suddenly stopped and a row of lights along the side of the table flashed on. The light illuminated her body and she could see more of the room.

The ceiling was concave. There was what looked like little white hockey pucks placed all over it, spread out evenly, about twelve inches apart. Lisa also noticed that there were small, round windows placed in the room. She could see four on each side of her, but could not see through them.

I became aware of a noise behind me. It was a soft, mechanical humming sound. I felt something push against the crown of my head and felt a pressure building in my ears. Two small, metal arms with large syringe-like protrusions came from somewhere out of my line of sight. The needles slowly moved forward perpendicular to my body, and then stopped and suddenly turned downwards directly above my eyes. I tried to squirm and fought against the thing that was holding my head in place, but I couldn't move. I couldn't even squirm. I was paralyzed. I tried to close my eyes, but even they wouldn't move. As the needles came closer to my eyes, I kept thinking that this has to be a nightmare. I willed myself to wake up, but the needles kept coming. I felt my bladder release. I could feel the warmth of my urine pooling around my legs and buttocks, and then the voices started murmuring again.

When Lisa woke up she found that she and the table had been cleaned. Thankfully, the needles that had once been poised over her head were nowhere in sight. She feared they would soon return, and she was right.

After I woke up and found that I had been cleaned and saw that the needles were gone, I had a momentary sense that everything was going to be alright. They could do anything they wanted to me as long as they kept those damn needles away from my eyes. I didn't care if they did sexual things to me or even killed me; I just didn't want to see those needles.

I became aware of that familiar mechanical buzz behind me again. The voices started just about the time I saw the needles coming overhead. I cried out, I tried to think of anything to keep them away from me. I thought if urinating on the table worked once I would try it again. As hard as I tried nothing would come; I was empty. As the needles started their downward progress once again, I screamed, but no sound came out of my vocal chords. I could hear the voices again, mumbling in the background. They were talking faster as the needles approached my eyes. I tried to close them, but couldn't. It was like they had paralyzed the parts of me they didn't want to move. I prayed, but God wasn't listening.

What happened to Lisa next are the ingredients of nightmares. The needles did keep coming. The needles punctured her eyeballs with a loud popping sound. Lisa claims she felt every bit of this. The needles punctured the lens of her eyes, then her corneas where the needles came to rest. She felt a small vibration as if the needles were oscillating in an up-and-down motion, or drilling deeper into her optic nerve. The voices were quiet now, no sounds except for the small mechanical whir inside her head. She tried to scream again, but her vocal chords were still paralyzed. Once again, she willed herself to wake from this nightmare. Once again, her will failed her. This was not a nightmare. It was reality, much worse than any dream could ever have been. There was no waking from this horror.

The whirring finally ceased and the needles started to rise once again, withdrawing themselves from her eyes; in an instant she could see blurry outline of the room. Then she went blind. She could see nothing. The horror of what was happening to her kept building.

> I couldn't see anything. The first thoughts I had were of my family. Was I ever going to see them again? Even if I made it out of this alive, would I be blind for the rest of my life? The voices started up again, slowly then more frantic as if an argument was taking place. Then I felt a warm, sticky liquid on both sides of my cheeks. I was perplexed at first, until I smelled the sickly, irony smell of blood. Then I knew what it was: My eyes were bleeding and the blood was running down the side of my face. That's why I couldn't see. When the needles retracted, my eyes started to bleed and the blood was blocking my vision. I was able to blink again, and I blinked furiously trying to clear my vision. It started to clear just as I felt myself falling asleep. But it wasn't sleep; they were making me unconscious again. The last thought before the world went black was: Will I wake up this time?

When Lisa woke up she was in a different room. She was twisting her head around to see what was around her when she realized she was no longer immobilized. She sat up on the edge of the white table which she had been laid upon. She was naked. The room was large, approximately 30'x30'. Except for the table she sat upon, it was empty. The ceiling and floors were a stark white with a sheen to them that made them look wet. The walls were entirely covered in mirrors. From floor to ceiling and all around the room, it was one seamless mirror.

Remembering the needles, she put her hands up to her eyes to see if she was still bleeding. There was no blood and she felt no pain. Lisa got to her feet and began walking around the room looking for a door. Not finding one, she began to beat her fists on the mirrored wall. The murmuring voices started again. The voices surrounded her, coming from every direction and no direction all at once. She began to scream as loud as she could.

> I wanted out of that room. I wanted to go home, so I went a little crazy. I screamed at the walls. I beat on the mirrors. I flailed, I kicked. I even cursed my unseen captors,

The spot where Lisa was abducted by aliens.
Photo Courtesy of: Angela Turney.

all to no avail. When I was completely exhausted, I just sank to the floor and started crying. When I couldn't make them understand me with rage, I tried pity. The voices stopped.

Suddenly, Lisa felt a presence in the room with her. She turned to see a small, grayish creature standing about ten feet behind her. The being was no more than four feet tall. It had large eyes and when it looked at her, it cocked its head in a curious manner. Surprisingly, Lisa was not frightened. She was more astonished than anything else. She had seen people on television who claimed they were alien abductees and the creature that was now before her was exactly how many of those people had described them to be. The long arms that extended into long fingers were attached to a dusky, gray body. It shuffled towards her a few steps and she instinctively jumped up and ran to the other side of the room. The creature stopped and gave another curious look. Then it spoke to her. Not in the way humans speak— it spoke inside her head.

She kept hearing the word "Why." Lisa spoke back.

"Why, what?" She asked.

"Why?"

"I don't know what you're asking," she answered back in her head.

"Why are you frightened?"

"You hurt me, you kidnapped me."

"It was necessary," it answered.

"Hurting me was necessary?"

"Yes."

"Why?"

"To learn."

"To learn what?" she asked.

"How to save your species."

"Save us from what?"

"Yourselves."

With that, Lisa felt herself beginning to pass out again. She woke up sitting in her car. She looked at the clock on her car radio and realized she had only been gone for three hours. Her cell phone was buzzing a voice mail alert. Her friend, whom she was supposed to have met earlier in the night, had called her several times. Lisa sat in her car staring out through the windshield, trying to make sense of what had happened to her. "Yourselves," kept popping into her mind. What did it mean by that? She thinks about that question every day.

I asked Lisa how her life has changed since her abduction and she told me that she spends most of her free time researching alien abductions. She is obsessed with getting answers.

> I want to know why they did this to me. I mean, what was the larger purpose? I don't understand how putting needles into my eyes is going to help save humanity. But, from what I've read, that seems to be the constant in these abductions. Almost everyone who has been abducted has reported some type of medical experimentation, or test being conducted on them. Ya know, it's funny; I drive down the road where I was abducted almost every day. Sometimes I pull over and think about what happened to me; other times I drive by without giving it a second thought. I've gotten used to it. My life has been forever changed, not for better or worse, just different. I have a knowledge of something now that most people think of as hoax or something some crazy person says happened to them. Now, I know it's real. I experienced it. I remember it. That's something the skeptics and naysayers can't take away from me.

Lisa has not spoken openly about what happened to her. She keeps this secret close to her heart. When I asked her why she has not, at least, told her family, she just smiled and said, "How would you react if one of your family members told the story I just told you?"

Whatever your reaction is to this story, whether you choose to believe or not is up to you. However, the question must be asked: If alien abductions are just delusions of the insane and those seeking attention, then why are the majority of these abduction stories so similar? The descriptions of alien craft, the experiments, and the aliens themselves are all pretty much constant no matter who you hear them from. And what did they mean by saving us from *ourselves*? Are beings from another planet up there somewhere monitoring our progress as humans? This is a fair question; we are definitely a destructive species. When we are not destroying our planet, we destroy other things, like each other. The real question should be: Are we even worth saving?

Searcy is not hard to find. Take US 167/US 67 north out of Little Rock to Exit 42. Merge on to US 67 north to Searcy.

The House of Many Spirits

Many Spirits

Private Residence • Warren, Arkansas

When Warren was platted for city expansion, the city lots were laid out so that each home would have room for a small farm. Warren was to be a city based on agricultural views and the founding fathers felt that farming would be the best industry suited for the small city's survival. Other city planners with bigger connections felt differently and began to push for the lumber industry to settle in or close to Warren. By 1900, Warren became a lumber town and heavily depended on the construction industry for the survival of the populace. Today, Warren has a diversified economy and has grown to be a leader among small southern Arkansas communities.

Exterior view of the House of Many Spirits.

The House of Many Spirits is one of many beautiful antebellum homes in Warren. It has one unique characteristic that distinguishes it from all others. It was built in the center of the old town cemetery. It is believed that William Neely, one of the town doctors, built the house in 1880. Why he built it in a cemetery is unknown.

Over the years, some of the tombstones have been knocked over and some have disappeared to vandals. Of the ones that remain, the cemetery appears to be much older than 1880. It is rumored that when the construction began, the contractor simply pulled up the stones that got in the way of construction and threw them out in the side yard to be dealt with at a later date. The foundations of this mighty house were dug and laid over the graves of some of Warren's founding citizens.

Originally, the house was a small two-story home, but there is evidence of additions throughout the house. Closets were added during one renovation and indoor facilities during another. The kitchen and an upstairs studio were added also. During the most recent renovation, the house was re-wired, re-plumbed, and central air and heat were added.

Very few families have lived in the old house. It is believed that the original owner and his descendants lived there the longest. Recent history shows the house standing empty and boarded up. During this time of abandonment, the house saw its share of drug abuse, sex, fights, and even murder. When the owners left in 1963, they went in such a hurry that they left behind all of their furniture and belongings. They never returned for them; the house was boarded up and it stayed in this condition for almost forty years.

The family that finally bought the old house around 2004, sold all of the antique furniture, cleaned out the closets and renovated the house. They only lived in the house a short time before leaving abruptly. The house was put up for sale and finally sold to the current owners. The current owners, who wish to remain anonymous, started having trouble soon after they moved in. Things that could not be readily explained plagued them. It got so bad that they too have moved off, leaving behind all of their furniture and belongings.

Why are these people moving out in such a hurry? Is this house so haunted that no one can stay in it for any length of time? These questions and more were on the minds of the owners as they contacted me to come see if I could tell what was going on in their home.

A Haunted Property

When I first met the owner of the house I was headed to another paranormal investigation in Arkansas City. Jason and I were traveling on I-530 in our mobile research van when a car went by us rather quickly. We noticed the people were waving but we figured they were just being friendly. When we are on the road, this happens often, so we just waved and kept going. The car slowed down and the people inside started waving and pointing. This time we thought maybe something was wrong with the van so we pulled off the interstate as soon as an exit was available. They followed us and approached the van once we had stopped. It turned out that they were in need of our services. They had a haunting and the haunting was so bad that they were afraid to go home.

Unfortunately, we were headed to another city and would not be immediately available. The woman from the car understood, but informed us that she would not be going back to *that house* until we'd had time to check it out. Once a date was set, we headed to Warren for our first official meeting with the owners.

Our first meeting was with the owner of the house, one of her daughters, and a friend. The other members of the family were not available for an interview. The interview revealed that the owner had been having some bad times in the house. Soon after moving in, she started hearing and seeing little things that just did not seem right. She heard what sounded like someone walking around upstairs when she was the only one home. Small items, like a pencil or an earring, would come up missing.

One day, she went into an upstairs bedroom and found the covers to the bed neatly turned up from the bottom. Another time she went to the

Inside the house after the owners left, never to return. The contact with ghostly beings became so intense for the family, they left all furnishings and clothing behind. Much later, they hired people to remove their belongings.

same room and found the quilt that was on a chair turned up from the floor. These things always mystified her, but did not scare her. Numerous times while cleaning she would find coins on the floor or on a side table that had not been there earlier. In some cases, the coins were standing on edge. She heard doors open and close as if someone was going through them.

She was not alone when it came to experiencing supernatural happenings. Her husband started complaining about a shadow following him. On various occasions, he would look at the floor and see two shadows, one of himself and another shadow a little to the side of his. When he tried to show his wife his second shadow, it would move away and disappear. This really started to bother him. One morning, he asked his wife why she had covered him in the middle of the night. She told him that she had not. He was a very restless sleeper and never made his bed, but his wife often found his bed as if he had not slept in it.

One night, their son came home from a night out with his friends and went straight to bed. He was tired and had to get up early for work. Soon after getting to bed, his mother heard a crash from his room and then what sounded like someone running. She went to check on things and found her son in the bathroom looking at his back. He told her that he had been in bed and had just dozed off when a bottle of soda flew across the room and hit him in the back. He had a red whelp on his back and there was an open soda bottle lying on his floor by the bed.

Finally, the family had enough and began to move out one at time. First the son moved out, then one night, the husband was pushed by what he called his little shadow. He grabbed a few clothes and asked his wife if she was coming. They both left the house and have only recently hired people to go in and salvage their belongings. The only one who is comfortable in the house is the daughter. When I talked to her she said that she was not afraid, but that there were definitely ghosts in the house.

On Site

The rest of this story is being written while sitting on a hardwood floor in one of the upstairs bedrooms of what we first dubbed the *old cemetery house*. It is totally dark except for the light of the laptop computer and it is completely quiet. The time is about 12:15 a.m., and this is the only time I have ever written one of my stories at the location being haunted.

This photo was taken from the backyard toward the house.

It is very hard to explain what it feels like to be all alone in a room where spirit activity has been experienced. When the floor creaks, it causes a chill to run down my back. I sit wondering if I am truly alone.

The first time that I visited this house, I brought a small team of investigators with me to spend the weekend. I was looking forward to it and so was my team. We got there early enough to interview the owners, set up our usual equipment, and then wait. As our equipment recorded our every move, the house remained quiet. Although we recorded hours of video, took hundreds of photographs, and recorded lots of audio, we found very little proof of a haunting. We did get some strange audio recordings, but they were not of the caliber that would make me declare a house haunted. It was creepy and it was a general consensus that we had unseen visitors all night.

Sometimes when we visit an old house that is reported to be haunted, we do not find much at first. When we make repeated visits, the activity tends to pick up. It is like the spirits have to get to know us before they will make themselves known. The family had not moved out when we visited the first time, but when we went the second time, they were gone and would not come back to even et us in. The owner left a key with a neighbor for us to pick up when we got to town. It had gotten that bad for them in such a short time.

The second trip was a more productive trip. We arrived at the house around 8 p.m. and let ourselves in the back door. This time, I took enough investigators to cover the entire house all at one time. I assigned an investigator to each room in the house. I told them that they were to set up their equipment and spend the night in that room watching and taking lots of notes. By doing this, we were able to verify where the hot spots were. On this investigation, we saw some fast moving shadows, heard footsteps on floors where no one was walking, got a couple of good EVPs or disembodied voices, and in one picture, a person is shown sitting on the couch where no one was sitting. We also *recorded* the footsteps. They sounded like a male wearing boots, walking slowly across the wood floor. The most active spots were upstairs in and around the master bedroom.

We are now, at this writing, working the house for the third time. As I sit in this dark room waiting and listening, I see an unhappy house. I am sitting in the room where the image of a person was captured on film sitting on the couch. The couch is long gone, but I feel that the person is not. This house never had a chance to be a home. It is surrounded by death and was the residence of a medical doctor.

On this investigation, I have brought our team medium. It was she who finally gave this story a name. She told me that this house has many spirits in it. While interviewing her, I noticed that she had two shadows. One of the shadows was jumping around as if trying to get my attention. I told her about the other shadow and she started looking around the room. By cutting her eyes first right then left she was able to tell me that we had company to her left. When we turned to look, we both saw a shadow person but only for a brief moment. When the shadow person disappeared, I looked back at her and her second shadow was gone. Later that night, we heard walking in the room and lots of voices. The voices were so numerous that we could not make out any details.

As I sit here waiting, I can hear the sound of heavy footsteps coming toward me. I am alone or at least no one living is in the room with me. The psychic is downstairs asleep. The footsteps are getting closer. If they do not stop, they will walk through me or have to go around as I am blocking a door. The footsteps have stopped for now; they stopped within inches of where I am sitting. I feel like I am being watched. There they go again on the other side of me. The spirit must have stepped over my legs to continue to wherever it was going. The sound of footsteps fade and have now stopped again. Interestingly, I still feel as if I am being watched. Chills are running down my back.

A Review

After a review of all of the data and personal stories concerning the House of Many Spirits, we have come to understand what may be going on in the house. The house was built in the late 1800s, but the cemetery in which it is built existed long before that. The spirits of the cemetery have taken over the house. It is theirs and any living human who enters is an intruder into their world. The spirits are not interacting with their human counterparts to run them out, but rather ignoring the fact that humans exist in their house. Thus the living feel uneasy and not welcome in their own home. They just want to get out as fast as they can and do so often, leaving behind their personal belongings. The House of Many Spirits is very haunted and will always remain so until it no longer exists.

Warren is a quiet little town in southwest Arkansas; to get there you take I-530 south out of Little Rock. Travel about 43 miles and merge onto US 63 south for another 42 miles. That should do it. Look for the house sitting in the middle of a cemetery but remember this is a private residence and the owners would not welcome visitors.

Demon Be Gone

Scott, Arkansas

"It's inside me! I can feel it, make it stop!"

This is the cry that came from a teenage girl in the small town of Scott, Arkansas. The thing inside her was a black presence that tortured the girl and her family for several months, ripping her flesh and shredding her mind until there was only one solution left...an exorcism.

Katherine Jenson, known as Kat to her friends, was brought up in a normal, God-fearing, southern home. Kat was Pentecostal, and all that came with this particular faith. She wore her dark, red hair, long. She favored skirts over pants and thought makeup was for clowns and children. She had complete faith in God, but rarely thought about Satan, until he sent her a reminder of his presence.

Acting Out

It was spring 2004; the cold weather was on its way out, and the sunshine was beginning to wake the flowers and trees from their slumber. The first sign that something was wrong happened one night at church. Sitting in the pew, listening to the sermon, Kat became violently ill. She ran to the ladies' room and vomited several times until the dry heaves overtook her and she lay on the tiled floor of the restroom crying, convulsing, and holding her stomach. Her mother, who had followed her when she ran out of the sanctuary, knelt beside her child and tried to soothe her. When the heaves started to subside and Kat could stand, her mother took her to the emergency room. There she was diagnosed with food poisoning and sent home with medicine and instructions to drink plenty of fluids and to get some rest.

A few days later, Kat's symptoms subsided and she felt well enough to return to school. Everything was normal for two weeks. Then, one day, Kat's mother, Elaine, received a phone call at work that her daughter had been taken by ambulance to the hospital. The school official gave little info, saying only that Elaine needed to get to the hospital as fast as she could. When she arrived at the emergency room, an attendant took her back to where Kat was being treated.

> When I walked in to where Kat was, my first thought was that she had been shot. There was blood everywhere. Her hair was matted to her head with blood, and I could barely make out the face of my little girl beneath all that blood.

Elaine started screaming at the nurses, "What happened to my daughter."

When the nurses were finally able to calm her down, they explained that Kat had several large contusions to her head and face and all the blood made it look worse than it actually was. No one at the hospital would tell Elaine exactly *how* Kat had received the massive cuts and bruises that covered her head and face. While sitting next to her unconscious daughter, a police officer came into the room and began to explain how Kat received her injuries.

Several students witnessed Kat's "accident." The police officer, reading from his note pad, told Elaine that between second and third periods, Kat was walking to her next class when she suddenly stopped in front of a row of metal lockers and began smashing her head into them repeatedly. Blood was flying everywhere as students tried and failed to hold Kat down and stop her from hurting herself. One student who had tried to grab hold of her said Kat elbowed her in the nose and threw her to the ground, then continued slamming her head into the locker. It took three teachers and a school resource officer to finally drag her away from the lockers and into the school's nurse's station, a bloody trail behind them. The officer could offer no explanation as to why Kat did this to herself.

Elaine sat in silence beside her daughter trying to figure out why her once normal, happy child would harm herself. As Kat lay unconscious, her friends and family stood in a circle around her bed, held hands, and prayed.

Two hours later, Kat woke up and asked her mother where she was. When Elaine explained to her what had happened, she replied, "No, I didn't do that!" Kat told her mother that she was walking down the hallway when she was pushed into the lockers from behind. Kat said she felt someone grab her shoulders and slam her into the lockers. She said she tried to put her arms out in front of herself to try to stop whoever was doing it, but she was not strong enough; she fought back until she was exhausted and passed out.

The story Kat gave to her mother was in complete contrast to what the dozens of witnesses described seeing. Kat says she passed out while still being slammed into the locker while everyone who witnessed the incident said she was awake, eyes open, and screaming her own name. Furthermore, the three teachers and the officer who managed to pull her away from the lockers said that she screamed and spit at them until they got her into the nurse's station where she passed out.

However, there was this: As the medical staff was examining her injuries to document them, they found something strange. Starting at her shoulders, down both sides of her back, were three, long, bloody lines that looked like claw marks extending down to the middle of her spine.

Nobody that witnessed the incident could explain how the marks had gotten there. Certainly, Kat would not have been able to reach around to where the marks were and do it to herself. These wounds had to have been made by someone else, but no one else was seen close to her when the "attack" occurred. There were no answers. The doctor suggested to Elaine that a mental evaluation should be conducted. Reluctantly, she agreed.

Kat spent two weeks at an inpatient mental facility while doctors tried to discover what caused her to act out and hurt herself. The claw marks were ignored. At the end of the two weeks, they had no answers and Elaine took her daughter home. At home, she tried the only therapy she believed could help her daughter, she prayed. The pastor of their church made several visits to their home over the next few months, but things only got worse.

Eventually, Kat was removed from school for acting out. She would stand up in the middle of class and curse the teachers and other students. She quit practicing basic hygiene, she went days without a shower, and almost never washed her hair. One day, Kat was sitting in science class. The teacher was lecturing, and in the middle of class, in front of everyone, Kat stood up, walked up to the teacher, raised her skirt, squatted down, and began to urinate on the floor while pointing and laughing. Elaine was summoned to the school and Kat was expelled for the remainder of the year.

Elaine was understandably furious with her daughter, and at the same time, terrified by what was happening to her. A few months earlier, she had a perfectly normal teenage child who was polite, went to church, and was a joy to have around. Now she had an insolent, mean child who paid no attention to her parents, or anyone else, for that matter. Elaine was at her wits end. She called her pastor and arranged for him to come over one night so they could confront Kat and try to get to the bottom of why she was acting like this.

The Jensons took their daughter, Kat, to an old country church for the demon exorcism.

Bringing in the Big Guns

That next night, Elaine, John, Kat's father, and Brother Jim, the pastor from their church, went up to Kat's room to plead with her to change her ways and explain herself. At first, when they opened her bedroom door they did not see her, and then they saw her feet sticking out from underneath her computer desk. She had crawled under the desk and sat there in a ball with her knees tucked against her chest. She was naked, and she had cuts all over her body. The cuts were actually carvings. They read… "Baal."

Baal is a Christian demon. He is purported to be the right hand of Satan or Beelzebub. He is a high-ranking demon, one who commands sixty-six legions of lesser demons, according to demonologists. Baal is often times depicted as a toad, sometimes a toad with spider's legs. He is one of the most powerful demons in Christianity and is said to be able to make those who summon him invisible, and with him, he carries the ashes of Hell in his pockets.

Next to Kat's feet lay a small, bloody screwdriver. She had used it to carve the demon's name into her arms, legs, stomach and finally onto her forehead. She sat there staring at the trio that had just entered her room. Then she smiled, and before Brother Jim could react she jumped out from under the desk and straight at him, bloody screwdriver in hand. She wrapped her legs around his waist and tried to climb on top of his shoulders, all the while swinging the screwdriver at his head trying to stab him. He tried to fight her off, but she "had the strength of ten men," he later said.

Kat's mother and father frantically wrestled with their child as they tried to pull her off the pastor. Kat swung the screwdriver wildly and stabbed her mother in the arm. Elaine let out a cry but did not let go. John tried to wrap his arms around her chest and pull her backwards onto the floor, but she was slippery from all the blood that ran from the carvings on her body and he could not get a grip on her. He pulled with everything he had and called out to God for help, His arms slipped again and he fell backwards, hard. He looked over and saw the pillow that lay on his daughter's bed. He quickly pulled the pillowcase off the pillow, ran up behind his naked, bloody daughter, and put the pillowcase over her head. She screeched and clawed at the fabric that was covering her head. This gave Brother Jim a chance to pry her legs from around his waist and he pushed her to the floor while her father held the pillowcase over her head. She had dropped the screwdriver and Elaine grabbed her daughter's arms and tried to restrain her. Finally, Kat succumbed to exhaustion and quit fighting. She lay there, pillowcase over her head while three terrified and completely spent adults stared at each other in disbelief.

Kat fell into a sort of stupor, or light sleep, and the three adults lifted her up and placed her onto her bed. As she lay in the bed, she began to whisper in tongues as she slowly moved her head from side to side. Eventually, she stopped and fell into a deep sleep while Elaine and the two men sat around the bed, prayed, and discussed what to do next. They could come up with only one solution. The demon had to be exorcised.

Kat lay unconscious for two days. Never doing more than barely opening her eyes and looking around and then falling back into unconsciousness, her parents and Brother Jim decided it would be safer to conduct the exorcism inside the church and that they would move her while she was still asleep. Praying she would stay asleep for the short trip, the three loaded her into the car and drove to the church.

When they arrived there were two church elders waiting for them. They unloaded Kat and carried her inside, placing her atop the alter. The five adults, led by Brother Jim, prayed while holding hands in a circle around Kat. When they finished their prayer of protection, Brother Jim began the exorcism:

In the name of Jesus!
I command you to leave this girls body!
I cast you out in the name of Jesus!
Out! Out! Out! Out!

At this point Kat began to writhe. Her eyes remained closed, but she was whimpering like a child in pain.

I cast you out in the name of Jesus!
I cast you out in the name of Jesus!
Out! Out! Out! Out!

Kat began to swing her head back and forth and she started to foam at the mouth. She spit green bile at Brother Jim as he continued to chant, louder and louder. She arched her back and screamed, but it was not her voice. It was a coarse, hideous voice and it began to laugh hysterically, and then Baal spoke to them:

Your God has no power over me
I cannot be commanded. I am Baal!

Brother Jim continued his chant:

I cast you out in the name of Jesus!

The demon only laughed and again spit its foul bile at the pastor. Brother Jim did not cease his commands. He continued:

In the name of God I command you to leave this girl!
In the name of Jesus!
I command you to leave this girl!
Out! Out! Out! Out!

Suddenly, Kat arched her back so hard Elaine was sure she was going to snap in two. The girl screamed and her arms shot straight out from her body, and her eyes rolled back into her head. She began to convulse and started talking in tongues. As she spoke the ancient language, Brother Jim was commanding the demon out, louder and louder now. Kat began twisting and turning in every direction. And as suddenly as it had started, it was over. A sharp whooshing sound was heard and then the breaking of glass. Kat lay still, no longer moving. She was taking shallow breaths and seemed to be sleeping. Kat's parents drove her home where she stayed in bed recovering for several days. When she finally awoke, she did not remember a thing about what had happened to her.

To this day Katherine remembers very little about those several months she was possessed. Her parents told her most of what she knows. She has a hard time accepting the fact that an actual demon had taken over her body and mind. She still visits Brother Jim and he has helped her understand and deal with what happened to her. Today, she is a well-adjusted college student who is about to graduate with a degree in teaching. Her external wounds have healed. Her mind is strong and she is grateful to God for saving her from the demon.

The only evidence that Baal left behind was a broken, stained-glass window that Baal shattered while leaving Kat's body and fleeing the church. When Kat's parents carried her out to the car that night they looked up at the window that had been shattered. Then, there on the ground, they saw the shattered glass; every shard had been stacked in neat little piles all in a row, by an unseen, banished demon on his way back to Hell.

From Little Rock, take I-440 east for about 7 miles to Exit 138. Merge on to US 165 east toward England. Scott is about 5 miles on down the road. The old church has been torn down, but believe me, the Devil still exists everywhere.

Anna

Prairie Grove Battlefield State Park
Prairie Grove, Arkansas

Not everyone can see her, but on a cold December evening Anna made her appearance to two unsuspecting Civil War re-enactors. Her outline could be seen moving about the empty historic structure of the place she once called home. Ben and Victor could not believe their eyes as they watched the ghost of Anna Borden peer at them from an upstairs window.

Prairie Grove, located deep in the Boston Mountains of Northwest Arkansas, is a quiet and peaceful little town. Like many seemingly peaceful places in the South, however, it has known war. On December 7, 1862, Confederate and Union forces descended on the little hamlet for a fierce one-day battle. The fate of northern Arkansas and southern Missouri lay in the balance, winner takes all, and an unassuming farmhouse was at the center of the fighting.

The Borden House

A small, two-story wooden farmhouse, the Borden House, was first seized by Confederate forces, which used it as an observation post to direct artillery. Later, Union forces took control of the house, then lost it, then captured it again. In an after-action report, it was stated that dead and dying lay all around the Borden House, and 250 bodies were counted within a 100-yard radius of the front door. One soldier reported that the ground was muddy with blood, and that a man would be hard pressed to walk to the house without stepping on a fallen comrade.

According to local legend, one of the Borden family's young sons, just 13 or 14 year old, slipped away during the battle to join the fight against the Yankees. The battle surged back and forth all day. As night fell, Confederate forces withdrew from the field, and the boy's mother and young siblings went out with lanterns, searching among the dead and wounded for the son who had run away to fight. It was days later that the boy's body was found, less than a mile from the house. He had been shot through the chest, and was laying face down in a ditch with the family rifle still clutched in his hands. He was only one of the 2,700 men counted as casualties in the days that followed, a total that included hundreds who died, and many more who watched their limbs sawn away by surgeons in a makeshift field hospital erected in the orchard behind the Borden House.

Our paranormal investigation group, Spirit Seekers, had heard rumors that the house and orchard were haunted, so we set out to see for ourselves. We chose the weekend of 142nd anniversary of the battle, with a re-enactment of the Prairie Grove engagement scheduled for the day we were to investigate.

An exterior view of the old Borden House where Anna was raised.

We arrived at the park and were greeted by an amazing sight: tents, open fire pits, horses, cannons, Yankees, and Rebels.

The battlefield itself is usually open to the public during the day, but the Borden House is kept locked at all times. Since we had received permission to investigate from Arkansas State Parks, the staff was very accommodating, and agreed to let us spend the night in the Borden House. For the rest of the day, we met with re-enactors. Once they heard about our pursuit of the paranormal, and why we were there, they were anxious to tell us about ghostly experiences at Prairie Grove.

While much of what we heard around the campfire fell squarely in the realm of a good yarn, one of the tales that afternoon peaked our curiosity; mostly because it confirmed another story we had heard earlier about the Borden House.

Keeping the Lights On

During a previous reenactment weekend at the battlefield, a re-enactor told us that he and a friend were returning to their tents after a Saturday evening dance, when they saw a light in the window of the Borden House. From the outside, the light seemed to be a candle or lantern—a bright, round, yellow orb that moved from window to window as they skirted the edge of the yard. It seemed as if someone inside the house was watching them as they walked. Knowing the house was locked up tightly, and with every history buff on the battlefield that night knowing better than to light a fire of any kind within a hundred yards of the wooden house, they knew it had to be the famed Borden House ghost.

Once Inside...

As dusk drew across the battlefield, we became more and more excited about the night's investigation. At twilight, the park superintendent appeared with the key and opened the door of the house. Once we were inside, he wished us good night, and locked the door behind us. At the click of the latch, the prearranged hour when he would return to let us out seemed days away. As the darkness of the house settled about us, I heard one of our fearless ghost hunters say, "I hope there aren't any mice in here." Luckily for her, it was so dark that if there *had* been a mouse, she wouldn't have seen it.

Keeping with the rustic theme of the battlefield, Borden House has no modern utilities. Every piece of our equipment had to be battery powered, so our time was limited. We divided up the duties and began the investigation. Tina was checking for temperature changes with the digital thermometer and later tried to record electronic voice phenomena—the voices of spirits, captured on audio tape. Angie and Rose, our psychic sensitives, were taking photographs and digital video, while casting about for psychic energy. I had a 35mm camera, and relieved the others of their equipment as needed.

Once things were quiet, our electromagnetic frequency meters began to show some activity around the steps leading to the upper level. The EMF meter measures electronic activity in the area, and there is a theory that spirits emit EMF while attempting to manifest. That being said, there are lots of potential sources of electromagnetic fields—the most common of which is the presence of shorts or bad connections in household electrical wiring. Given that there was no electrical wiring running to the house, the spikes were especially interesting.

An investigative photo taken in the house. The investigator was sitting on the steps when she had a feeling that Anna was close. This bright orb never left her side as she moved about the house. *Photo courtesy of Spirit Seekers Paranormal Investigation Research and Intervention Team (SPIRIT).*

Angie sat down on the steps about halfway between the landing and the second floor. Here, she was contacted by the spirit of a young girl named Anna, who had lived in the house and was interested in our presence. The cameras recorded paranormal activity all around the steps during and after the encounter. While watching the LCD screen as I took pictures, I could see that Angie was not alone. One very bright orb hovered in front of her face, barely three feet away, and seemed to be very interested in her, and what she was saying. Although Angie could not see the orb, and had no idea one was so close, it was with her the entire time she was sensing the spirit presence. When she moved, it moved.

After this encounter ended, I was preparing to move the equipment when I had my encounter with something supernatural. It could have been the same spirit that Angie had just encountered. I have a pencil attached to a retractable cord on my vest, so that I will not lose it in the dark. While standing at the foot of the stairs, the pencil and its cord were suddenly pulled out about eighteen inches from my chest, then let go. Unfortunately, as with most paranormal events, this strange event was not captured on film. Cameras are almost never pointing *where* they should be, *when* they should be.

Later, Rose and Angie sensed the presence of an older man in the downstairs family room. They said he was not happy that we were in his house. They asked him who he was, but he just sat in his chair and frowned at them, as he let them know he was displeased with the actions of one of his children. As they turned to leave the room, they came in contact with a third spirit. It was close to the back door and would not leave the area. This spirit indicated that it was sorry for something it had done and was afraid of the older man in the front room. Later, we found out about the boy who snuck out to join in the battle, and suspect this explains what was going on in the parlor between the two male spirits; one being angry, and one being sorry.

Finally, the park superintendent's key rattled in the lock. We left tired, but still excited about all we'd experienced during the night. I had film to develop, recordings to listen to, digital pictures to look at, video to review, and EMF data to evaluate, before we could report on our findings. We actually knew ery little about the history of the house before the investigation. All we knew vas that it had been in the middle of a Civil War Battle, and that the builder vas named Borden. The next morning, however, park officials gave us a very letailed account of the families who had owned the house. One of the people vho lived in the house, we learned, was a girl by the name of Caldonia Ann 3orden. Ann was nine years old when the battle took place and had very clear nemories of the battle and the days that followed. She died in Prairie Grove, . very old lady. Her memories of that day never faded.

During an interview with this re-enactor, an energy orb made n appearance. *Photo courtesy of Spirit Seekers Paranormal nvestigation Research and Intervention Team (SPIRIT).*

Evidence Review

Days later, while reviewing our photographic evidence, we recalled the campfire story the re-enactors told. One of the 35mm photographs, taken just before we entered the house that night, captured what appeared to be a yellow light in a second-floor window. We were all outside of the house at the time the photograph was taken, and the doors were still locked. There were no outside lights to cause a reflection, and nothing inside to cause a light. The shape of the light is oval, like the flame on a candle. Could this be the ghost of little Anna walking from window to window in search of her lost brother?

We left the Borden House knowing we had all been at the center of some sort of paranormal activity that evening. As we do with every haunting, we try o verify our findings; and in this case, the research helped to verify what we had seen and heard in the Borden House. That night, we walked off the battlefield hoping that whatever spirits roam there eventually find a final resting place, and the peace that eluded them in life.

The Borden house is protected and located in the middle of Prairie Grove Battlefield State Park. It is another fun place to visit and have a family outing. Prairie Grove Battlefield State Park can be found in northwest Arkansas. To get there from Little Rock, take I-40 west toward Fort Smith. After 141 miles take Exit 12 onto I-540 north headed toward Fayetteville. Take Exit 53 onto AR 170 north and go about 12 more miles. The park is just ahead.

Lake Conway
MONSTER

Lake Conway
Conway, Arkansas

The woods that surround Lake Conway, in Faulkner County are home to many types of species: mostly birds, snakes, raccoons, and the like. The lake itself boasts some of the best fishing in the state. Anglers come from all over to try and charm those bass and crappie onto their hooks and into their boats.

The Skunk Ape

Rumor says there is another type of animal in and around the lake, one no man will try to catch. After dark, the fishermen talk about it in low tones and look over their shoulders into the surrounding dark woods. Most do not speak its name for fear it may hear the call and appear. Those who do speak its name call it the Skunk Ape.

Modern sightings began in 1970. People started to call in to game wardens and local law enforcement and report strange sightings of something that looked like a man, but wasn't a man, living in the lake. Most eyewitnesses described the creature as being approximately seven to eight feet tall and ape-like. The creature is often sighted in the shallow areas of the lake looking for food. The sightings are always accompanied by an incredible stench coming from the creature, which is where it gets its name.

A Boating Scare

One incident in particular is especially disturbing. On a balmy August evening in 1985, Lee Allan was sitting in his flat-bottom boat, just about to pull up his line and head inland when he heard a sound behind him. Lee turned to see a large disturbance in the water about thirty yards away from where he was. Something in the water was thrashing around as if it had been submerged on a troutline; at first, Jim just thought it was a beaver that had become entangled in someone's trotline. Looking closer he realized that it was not a beaver he had spotted. It was much too large and hairy for it to have been just a beaver. As Lee sat in his boat staring at the object in the water, the monster stood upright. What he saw next was something that could come straight out of a Stephen King novel. Lee estimated that the water was about five feet deep where the creature was standing and there was still at least three to four feet of it showing above the water line.

The creature stared at Lee for a moment, as if it was equally surprised to see him, as Lee was to see it. The man and the creature locked eyes for what seemed like eternity, according to Lee. Suddenly, the creature started to move closer to Lee's boat, grimacing and making small guttural noises as it made its way. Lee was frozen with fear; he could not move or scream, he could only watch in horror as the monster came closer and closer, never once taking its eyes off Lee.

As the monster got closer, Lee's nostrils were assaulted by the horrendous smell that emanated from the creature. This shock to his senses was enough to bring him out of his stupor and force him into action. Lee turned to grab the .22 pistol he always carried with him to scare away snakes. As Lee turned back to aim the gun at the monster, he realized he had been to slow. While Lee had been fumbling around in the boat looking for the gun, the monster had quickly covered the distance to the boat, and as Lee swung his arm around, the monster knocked Lee out of the boat.

Lee came up from the water, gasping for air and reaching for something to grab hold of to regain his balance. He grabbed the side of the boat and slowly pulled himself up enough so he could see over the edge. The monster was still there but it was not paying attention to Lee anymore. The creature was focused on the stringer of fish Lee had caught earlier and had left hanging over the side of the boat. It pulled the stringer from the water and eyed the fish with a hungry gaze. One by one, the monster pulled the fish from the stringer, ripping the fish apart at the gills as it went. Lee watched the creature eat the fish whole, taking only two bites to consume an entire fish. Lee sat in the water watching in silence and fear. He worried that if he tried to make a break for it while the creature was devouring its meal that it would immediately attack him. Having little choice in the matter, Lee quietly tread water, and waited there and watched, hoping the creature would just go away after it had finished its meal. There would be no such luck for Lee on this day.

As the monster finished off the last fish, his gaze once again fell to the boat. Lee let go of the boat and tried to lower himself below the edge of it, careful not to make any sudden movements that would attract the attention of the creature. As Lee tried to stay as low in the water as he could without going under, he could hear the creature rummaging through the boat, slamming around the tackle box until it opened and, looking inside, obviously hoping for more food.

Suddenly, as Lee was grasping the side of the boat, it came up out of the water. The creature had seen the top of Lee's head poking up and reacted with sheer anger. The creature lifted the 300-pound aluminum boat as if it were made of cardboard. In just a split second, Lee was once again staring into the eyes of the beast. He had to act quickly if he wanted to live, and his only hope was reaching the shore and running for his life.

Lee turned in the water and headed for land. The shore was roughly seventy-five yards away; he half swam, and half ran through the water. Luckily,

This is a picture of the spot where Lee Allan emerged from the lake after fleeing from the monster. *Photo Courtesy of Gary Ivy.*

he was in the shallow part of the lake and he could use his feet to push off the bottom. Lee looked back only once, and he cried out in terror as he realized the creature was coming after him. He thought of his wife and children and tears streamed down his cheeks as he struggled through the murky water. He knew there was no way that he would be able to outdistance the creature, it was too strong and obviously very adept at being in the water. Behind him, Lee heard the creature rushing through the water, not sure how far behind it was, and not wanting to look back, he steeled himself and concentrated on getting to the shoreline.

His mind was racing. Lee wondered aloud what to do; he muttered a prayer, still moving through the water and briefly wondered what the authorities would tell his family had happened to him. One minute he was having a relaxing day, catching fish, watching the trees sway in the wind, and the next, he was being pursued by something from the depths of Hell.

Thinking only of survival at this point, Lee began to scream for help. He screamed as loud as his lungs would allow. If he was going to die he sure wasn't going to go out with a squeak,. Instead, he roared as loud as he could, hoping against hope that someone, somewhere close, would hear him. The shore was getting closer now, only twenty yards or so. His lungs were burning from screaming so loudly and trying to supply his body with needed oxygen at the same time. Lee's legs grew weak and he almost gave up and surrendered to the beast. Through pure fear, determination, and adrenaline Lee made it to the shoreline. He looked back towards the monster, and saw nothing but empty water behind him. The creature was nowhere in sight.

Lee lay there on the muddy bank of Lake Conway for a long while trying to make sense of what had just happened to him. He checked himself over and found no major injuries, save for one scratch that ran down his left cheek. He looked out over the open water trying to catch a glimpse of where the creature had gone. The only evidence that the monster had even been there was the capsized boat floating in the water and the debris that had been inside it.

This was not the only sighting of the Skunk Ape around the lake. Anglers often report feelings of being stalked as if something is just out of sight and is waiting for its prey (them) to walk into its trap. Most sightings happen just around dusk as most anglers are coming in from a day of fishing. Strange noises have been heard around the lake at odd hours. Some have even reported hearing the creature scream in the middle of the night as if celebrating a fresh kill. They say the scream the creature lets out will turn one's blood into ice water.

What Is It?

What exactly is the Skunk Ape? The scientific name for it is *hominid cryptid*. Hominid means: *great ape*, while cryptid means *a creature that cannot be scientifically proven to exist*. We know the creature exists. Reports of the creature were coming in almost constantly during the 1960s through the late 1970s. Most sightings were concentrated in the southeastern part of the country. Places like Florida specifically received numerous reports of the creature being sighted in the swamplands. The creature would sneak into populated areas at night and forage for food, sometimes stealing small pets during the night.

As recently as 2000, a photograph that purports to be that of a Skunk Ape was taken in Florida and sent to the Sarasota Sheriff's Department where the local press got a hold of it; and soon, sightings numbered in the dozens. The picture is that of a creature that is clearly ape-like standing on two legs peering out though the brush, eyes locked in a stare with the camera.

That the creature exists is a known fact to many around Lake Conway and the surrounding areas. Most locals will not even go outside after dark in certain parts of the lake. The creature tends to frequent the shallow part of the water, where it can easily slip into one of the many inlets that feed the lake. This could be why the creature is so hard to find; it has obviously been in the area for a very long time and would know the local terrain better than most of the residents.

Whatever the creature actually is may still be up for debate, but the argument that something is out there has already been won. Reported sightings still trickle in from time to time. So if you are brave enough, grab your fishing pole, a can of worms, and head out to Lake Conway...and hope the only thing that tugs on the end of your line is a hefty bass.

Lake Conway is just south of the city of Conway. To get there, take I-40 west out of Little Rock. It is only about 26 miles and home to some of Arkansas's best fishing. Be careful what you use for bait; you may catch something that cannot be thrown back.

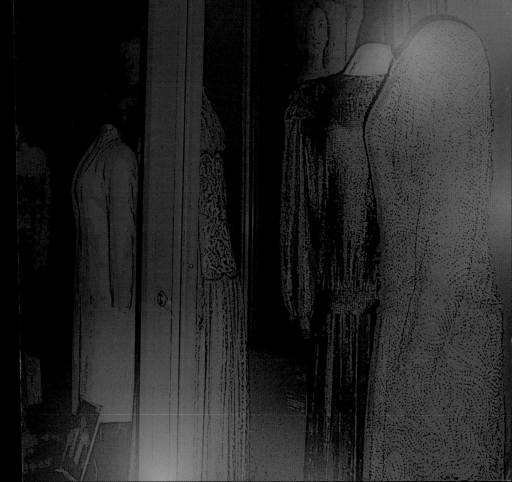

Order, Order in the House

The Old State House Museum
Little Rock, Arkansas

The Old State House.

Our federal government is founded on many good, solid principles. One such principle is freedom of speech. Little did the newly elected representative, J. J. Anthony, realize that freedom of speech would be the cause of his untimely death. Now his spirit roams the halls of justice in the Old State House Museum looking for his murderer.

The Old State House Museum is the oldest standing capitol building west of the Mississippi River. It is located on the Arkansas River in downtown Little Rock. The construction on the building started in 1833 and was completed in 1842. Although it was still under construction, government officials moved into the building when Arkansas became a state in 1836. The building served as our state capitol until 1911 when construction of the new capitol building was completed. The Old State House Museum has served Arkansans in many capacities over the years. It has been used as a facility to house federal and state offices, it was once a medical college, and today, it is a museum where all of Arkansas's history can be seen tastefully arranged in surroundings designed to teach all visitors.

The Old State House Museum has been the center of Arkansas history from early statehood days to current times. Soon after the building was occupied, two state representatives got into a knife fight on the floor of the small chambers.

.J. Anthony was killed in the fight. A short twenty-three years later, Arkansas voted to secede from the Union and join the newly formed Confederacy. The vote was taken in the very room where the knife fight had taken place. Soon after the War Between the States had ended, a political coup was attempted at this grand old building. Hundreds died in the attempt to oust the newly elected Governor of Arkansas as he sat in his office of the new east wing.

By the early 1900s, the state capitol moved to its new location and this building became a medical school. The Old State House fell into disrepair and the state attempted to sell it. It was rescued from destruction and made into a War Memorial. The building did not become a museum until 1947.

Its latest claim to fame is that it was here that Clinton announced his candidacy for the presidency, and here that he celebrated his victory on election night in 1992. During the weeks that followed, the spot Clinton characterized as his "favorite building in Arkansas," served as the stage for his cabinet appointments. On the evening of November 5, 1996, the Old State House once more became the center of the world's attention as President Bill Clinton became the first Democrat since Franklin Delano Roosevelt to be re-elected for a second term.

An investigative photo taken in one of the downstairs photo galleries. The bright energy orb is showing its ability to move about the room. Photo courtesy of Spirit Seekers Paranormal Investigation Research and Intervention Team (SPIRIT).

Rumors of Ghosts

There have been rumors of ghosts roaming the great halls of this beautiful building. Stories of apparitions showing themselves on the stairs and the sounds of a deadly knife fight have been reported in the small house chambers. Ladies dressed in homespun-cotton day dresses have been seen crowding the gallery area of the old House Chambers. An old slave woman has been seen sitting at the top of the winding staircase. The sound of a gavel pounding and a call to order has been reported.

Because of these stories and others, Spirit Seekers was allowed to spend the night in the Old State House Museum to gather evidence of a haunting or to dismiss the stories to an over-active imagination. We gathered at the foot

This is an investigative photo taken in the First Ladies' Gowns exhibit. Notice the shadow person captured hiding behind the last mannequin in the line. *Photo courtesy of Spirit Seekers Paranormal Investigation Research and Intervention Team (SPIRIT).*

of the spiral staircase where team assignments were made. I sent out the psychic team and waited for their return. Time passed slowly; it seemed that they were gone longer than usual. Upon their return, I interviewed them and found that they had picked up some psychic energy involving a few of the stories that I had been told.

Wooden Echoes

We set our equipment in the areas outlined by the team psychic in hopes of validating her findings. The evening's findings were impressive. We got some pictures of orbs as they streaked through the room. The most interesting find was on a voice recorder. While in the front chambers room upstairs, I was listening to the psychic explain what she was seeing and feeling. She was discussing how the room was charged with emotion, how the gallery was packed with citizens, as if waiting on an important announcement. The voices were all running together as if the room was full of talking people and the sound of a gavel pounding trying to get some order in the room was heard. When I listened to the recording, I could hear her talking, but in the background, there was a noise like a low murmur of voices. Then, as she said she could hear the pounding of a gavel, there was a hollow echo of wood striking wood. This is an amazing capture and validates the psychic's impressions of the activity surrounding that room.

The Staff Opens Up

While interviewing the staff, before the investigation, I found out that they were hesitant to tell me about things that had happened to them in the building. What is funny is that they all had stories to tell, but had not spoken of them because they did not want the other staff members to think them crazy. Once the evidence started to come in from the investigators, the staff began to open up. The stories started flowing and it became evident that all of them had been witness to some sort of paranormal event.

One lady told me that she worked late into the evening often. While at the old building she felt as if she was not alone. She said that when she went into a room to work on a display, the first few minutes were okay, but then it felt like someone, or something, had come into the room and was watching her. She always wrote it off as a bad case of nerves. She now believes that perhaps she was not alone. She said that knowing does not make it better and has caused her to reevaluate the idea of working late. She will not be working into the evening hours without a work partner anymore.

Another staff person related that, one evening, he had heard what sounded like a door slamming on the second floor. He was the security person on duty that evening, so he wanted to know more. He responded to the area from where he felt the noise had originated, but failed to find anyone in the building.

The entire building is monitored by security cameras. Once in awhile, the tapes are reviewed for quality. They are normally only reviewed if there is a problem in an area. Once, a shadow was seen that could not have been cast by a person. The guard responded to the area and found nothing.

Stop! Don't Go In There!

Other than psychic connections, there were a couple of times that investigators had experiences with the paranormal during the evening of investigations at the Old State House Museum. I was one of them. While on the second floor, close to an area the museum calls the First Families Gallery, I felt a presence that couldn't be described. For most of the State House's tenure as the seat of government, this suite of four rooms made up the Governor's Office. The room to the southeast was the waiting area. In the southwest corner of the suite was the governor's secretary. In the office to the northeast is where the governor received visitors, and the northwest corner office was the governor's private inner sanctum. Today, these same four rooms constitute the galleries of the First Families Exhibit. In these exhibits are artifacts from all of Arkansas's past governors and their families displayed for the public to see. It was in this area where I had my experience. I'm not sure that my experience could be classified as contact with a ghost, but it was definitely a paranormal experience.

I'd started to go into the suite of rooms when my little voice in my head said *STOP, don't go in there*. There was another little voice calling to me to *come in*. It was as if someone was saying, "Come over here; I want to show you something." But, I couldn't force myself to go in that suite of rooms. I found out later that one of my investigators had gone into the area and couldn't get out fast enough. He said that there was something in there that made him feel very uneasy.

When we were reviewing the data gathered from this investigation, we found a picture in that area that had a shadow person in it. It was the distinct outline of a full human torso standing close to the displays. The investigator who took the photograph was our team psychic and she told me that she felt that there was a spirit in the room with her at the time she took the picture. She said that the only time she takes pictures is when she feels that something is close.

There are times while walking through the museum a person may hear doors slam, or they may see a shadow cross their path, or maybe hear voices in the house chambers as a vote is taken to secede from the union is made, or a mysterious slave woman may appear and greet you on your way up the spiral stairs at the Old State House Museum. As you enter this building, be ready to experience history up close and personal. Be sure to say "hi" to Martha as you ascend the spiral staircase in the center of the building. She appears to be waiting for a decision to come out of the original House Chambers.

The Old State House Museum is located at 300 West Markham in Little Rock.

The Mena Poltergeist

Private Residence
Mena, Arkansas

Tucked in amongst the mountains of the Ouachita National Forest is the small town of Mena, Arkansas. The town was settled in 1896 as part of a rail line that ran between Fort Smith and Texarkana. It is a rural town that is defined by its agricultural and railroad roots. The county seat of Polk County, Mena, is a town of friendly, down-home folks. They work hard and are not prone to fanciful stories about ghosts or goblins in the night. Mention a ghost in one of the local diners and you're apt to get some strange looks, but not much more than that. Unless, you ask about the poltergeist; then you will get an opinion from just about everyone in town.

In December 1961, Mena became the focus of the entire state when it was reported that a poltergeist had taken up residence in the family home of Ed Shinn. The story immediately hit the news wires and was printed in almost every newspaper across the state. Shinn and his wife, Birdie, along with their fifteen-year-old grandson, Charles Shaeffer, had been run out of their home buy an unseen, angry spirit.

Ghostly Harassment

For more than a couple years, the Shinn family had been subjected to all manner of ghostly harassment. The first sign of activity was simple knocking on the walls when they were sleeping. Knocking that seemed to come from *within* the wall instead of the other side of it. Soon, other things began to happen, like sheets and quilts being ripped off of the bed while Ed and Birdie were still awake. Ed often investigated and found nothing that could explain what had happened.

The family learned to live with these encounters for a while, not wanting to say anything and be thought fools; they hoped the unseen prankster would disappear as quickly as it had appeared. The family had no such luck.

The activity only increased. Soon, there were dishes and kitchen utensils being thrown about. The knocking of the walls moved to the windows, shaking the glass in the frames so hard that Birdie thought every window in the house would shatter at any moment. At one point, a bag of marbles had been spilled onto the floor. Ed picked them up and placed them in another room only to walk out and find them scattered all around the living room floor. He again picked up the marbles, took them to the barn and dropped them between two bales of hay. That was the last of the marbles, but other household items soon began to fly around the house.

Mrs. W.E. Shinn, Ed's daughter-in-law, reported to have seen a coal bucket come flying through the air, aimed straight at her head; she avoided the flying bucket and it bounced off a wall and clanked to the floor, narrowly missing her.

Birdie's brother, Gene Whittenberg, witnessed a pencil floating in the air. He said it just hovered there like a bee over a flower, and then all of the sudden dropped to the floor.

Ed tried to keep the activity under wraps, but when he confided in a friend, the local butcher, the news soon spread beyond the town's sleepy confines and across the state. Local authorities got wind of the happenings at the Shinn farm and Sheriff Bruce Scoggin was called out to help. Scoggin brought two deputies, a trooper, and four reporters to the farm to stay the night and see if they could catch the spirit in action. The Shinns had fled the house earlier in the day and were staying with neighbors. The group of men stayed the entire night without seeing so much as a mouse. That led some to believe that the ghostly goings on may be a little more than just your average haunting. No one accused the family of making up the stories; everyone in town knew the Shinns were not liars or attention seekers. Attention soon focused on the grandson, Charles Elbert Shaeffer.

Strange Activity

Charles Shaeffer was fifteen years old, and like many young teenage boys when hitting puberty, he had plenty of pent up angst. Charles was not one of the popular kids in school; he was slightly overweight and was teased about it quite frequently. Teenagers can be cruel to one another and this can surely lead to rage and feelings of despair, not to mention frustration. All of these things combined with the natural changes taking place in a teen can come together in a kind of "perfect storm." This storm can lead to one of the most fascinating phenomena in the paranormal realm, the poltergeist.

Poltergeist is a German word meaning *noisy spirit or noisy ghost.* There are many theories on poltergeists and their causes but the prevailing theory is that they are caused not by a ghost or spirit but by a prepubescent child, usually a girl. There are, however, cases where a male child was thought to have been touched by these phenomena as well. The hormones and the changing physiology of a pre-pubescent child can sometimes bring about a kind of psychokinesis, meaning: *movement from the mind.* This is a very real phenomenon, one that has been documented in hundreds of cases.

The family soon went to stay with neighbors in hope that the ruckus would settle down while they were away. After a couple of days away from the farm, the Shinns returned home in hopes of having a quiet night. Again, no such luck. Neighbors who where there at the time witnessed the continuing harassment, such as biscuits flying off the kitchen table and slamming against the wall. One

At an old farmhouse near Mena, a poltergeist ruled the family with an unseen force.

neighbor, J.L. Ply witnessed a box of matches, carried by an unseen hand, cross the room where they were then thrown against the wall and spilled to the floor. Mr. Shinn was also physically assaulted by a figurine that flew off a shelf and hit him in the face.

Everyone involved in the case was at a total loss as for an explanation for the activity. Even the famous parapsychology department at Duke University was consulted, and while they did not conduct an actual investigation, according to the *Arkansas Gazette*, assistant director of the laboratory, J.G. Pratt, stated:

> It is the type of phenomena which recurs frequently. It challenges investigation in our field.

Mr. Shinn put forth another explanation. He believed that the activity could somehow be related to the, "…rockets and space ships and bomb tests." He was obviously referring to the atomic tests that had been taking place in New Mexico and other places prior to 1961. Could it have been just an overdose of radiation that was causing the activity? Maybe radioactive fallout from the Marshall Islands atomic tests that were carried out just three years before the activity stated? While it is true, there was radioactive fallout that made its way to Arkansas, there is no evidence that radiation can cause such effects.

A few days later Charles admitted to a reporter and one of the deputies that the entire thing had been created by him, that it was just a prank. He told reporters, and anyone who would listen, that he had caused all the problems because he was angry at his grandfather for yelling at him one night, and he wanted to get back at him by scaring him. To most, this seemed a plausible explanation and most people believed the boy, but there were others who still had questions and doubted this explanation.

Remaining Questions

Several questions remained. One seemingly obvious flaw in the young man's story was that several people had witnessed these events and they swore that there was no way the boy could have manipulated the flying objects without them being able to see him do it. This could leave only one explanation, that all of the neighbors, family, and friends had been complicit in a conspiracy to make people believe that the house was indeed haunted.

Could this actually be what happened in Mena all those years ago? The overwhelming answer from those who have studied the case and from those who witnessed it is a resounding, *no*! Young Charles could not have pulled this off without, at the very least, some help. Most people believe the boy was pressured by his grandfather—who was tired of all the publicity—to admit to the pranks so the family could return to a somewhat normal life. It's no secret the elder Shinn was uncomfortable with all of the reporters and the general public traipsing through his home as if it were a tourist attraction. Some people believe half of his story; they think some of the activity was paranormal in nature, but that the boy had also played a part in it to make it worse than it really was.

But, think about this: Could Charles actually have snuck into his grandparent's bedroom while they were still awake, pull the covers off of the bed and escape back into his own room before being discovered? Maybe once, but certainly not over and over again and how could he have made Bibles float across the room in front of several witnesses without being seen? The simple answer is that he couldn't have.

Then there were the voices that Mrs. Shinn heard while laying in bed. After one late night of activity, an exhausted Mrs. Shinn asked the "spirit" to be quiet. When that request was ignored, she asked it to just go to sleep. The response, according to the *Arkansas Gazette* was, "I don't sleep; you don't need to sleep either." Could the voice she heard have been that of her grandson? Possible yes, but it is not very likely that she would have failed to recognize his voice.

What about the rattling of the windows throughout the house? No fifteen-year-old boy I know can shake an entire house and make windows rattle. There are just too many holes in Charles' story for this to be washed away by a confession. It is more likely that Charles knew he was the cause of the activity, albeit in a paranormal nature that he himself did not even understand, so how could he have explained this to his family and the police?

There are many schools of thought on psychokinetic powers and some believe that the person who is manifesting the power is totally aware of what he or she is doing. It is entirely possible that Charles knew he controlled the power that was manifesting in his home, but he could do nothing to stop it. Like an involuntary muscle spasm, you know it's happening but trying to stop it is fruitless. The human mind is largely unknown to science in general. Sure, we know a lot more about the brain than we did in 1952, but we don't know entirely how it works. The brain is an enigma; it has taken us decades to understand what little we now know. To say absolutely, in the face of so much circumstantial evidence of psychokinesis that there is no possible way it can exist is pure arrogance.

So what ever happened to the Shinn family and young Charles? After the media circus died down, the family tried to settle back into as normal a life as they could. No other reports of activity were ever documented again at the house, which could be an argument for the camp that believes that it was all a hoax. However, it is more likely that even if the family had continued experiencing poltergeist activity in their house, it is unlikely they would have sought help or reported it. The family just wanted peace and quiet and to return to life as usual.

The question remains unanswered in many minds, even after all these years. There are still folks on both sides of the fence. Ultimately, the answer is that we will never truly know what took place in that small farm house in 1961. Was it real paranormal activity or just the pranks of an over-anxious teen trying to get back at his grandparents for being too strict? I will leave you with this last bit of information spoken straight from Charles' own lips. When asked why he decided to stop the pranks and admit to what he had been doing, he simply answered, "a voice" told him it was time to stop.

Mena is located in the west central part of Arkansas. To get there take I30 west out of Little Rock. Go west about 28 miles and take Exit 111 to merge onto US 70. Take US 70 west for about 13 miles, then merge onto US 270 west. Stay on US 270 west for about 64 miles, then start looking for US 71 north. Stay on US 71 north for about 21 miles to Mena.

He Lost His Head

Gurdon, Arkansas

The area where the infamous stretch of railroad crosses Highway 53.

As children, many of us believe that the boogieman hides in the dark corners of our rooms, or under the bed, or behind the bushes next to the house. As a result, many are afraid of the dark. But things are different in Gurdon, Arkansas. People there are afraid of the *Light*.

Gurdon is a small community located in the Southwestern part of Arkansas; and the citizens are mostly employed in the railroad or timber industries. The city was incorporated in 1880 and soon became the center of economic development in the region. Gurdon has a long and colorful history, and so does the Gurdon Ghost Light. The body of William McClain was found lying alongside a long, lonely stretch of railroad outside of Gurdon in 1931. While the murder of William McClain was being investigated, a local resident reported seeing a mysterious light waving back and forth on the railroad track in the same area. It is not actually known if McClain was killed there, or killed somewhere else and dumped by the tracks; but local residents think he was murdered where the body was found, because of the appearance of the light. The locals believe the light is the ghost of William McClain, walking the tracks between Sticky Road and Highway 53, in search of his missing head.

Several Versions Exist

Several versions of the life and death of William McClain exist and have been told over the years. However, they all agree that he was a foreman for the railroad, he was murdered, his headless body was found beside the railroad tracks, and his head was never found.

One story claims that McClain had fired an employee on the day of the murder and that the irate employee waited in the dark of the evening to kill him, as McClain made his final car inspection. Another story tells of a love triangle in which a jealous husband takes revenge by killing McClain, and dumps the body by the tracks in a remote area. Still another tale tells of an accident in which McClain is beheaded by a rolling boxcar.

However it happened, one question remains: What happened to his head? Did the killer keep the head as a trophy? Did wild animals carry the head off into the woods? Did the head get caught in the wheels of the train, only to be dislodged in another part of the State? The question seems to baffle everyone, including William. As mentioned, it has been suggested that the light often seen out on the tracks bobbing up and down, swinging to and fro, is actually a lantern carried by poor William as he walks the tracks looking for his missing head.

A Trip to the Light

The Spirit Seekers Paranormal Investigations Team gathers a couple of times each year to socialize. Our trip to see the Gurdon Light was to be one of these social events. What started out as a carefree walk on a cold winter's evening, turned out to be a full-blown supernatural investigation.

We had been out on the tracks for close to an hour, talking, taking pictures, and enjoying one another's company, when one of our psychics, Rose, whispered that someone or something was following us. I became alarmed and backtracked to make sure that we were not going to be harassed by local townspeople who might be out for a good time. I was warned that this could happen if word got out that we were on the tracks hoping to see the Light. But I found nothing and returned to the rest of the group.

Confident that we were not being followed, I supposed that perhaps Rose was wrong, and she had misinterpreted her feelings. As we continued along the tracks, Rose kept insisting that someone or something was following us. Between trestles three and four, we stopped and took some pictures behind

When one of my investigators told me someone was following us, I turned and took this photo. Notice the blue outline of a person crossing the tracks, it has no head. *Photo courtesy of Spirit Seekers Paranormal Investigation Research and Intervention Team (SPIRIT).*

us in hopes of catching something in the flash; and much to my surprise, found that we *were* being followed. The digital camera screen showed the figure of a person crossing the tracks. A full torso with legs and arms could be seen plain as day, but no head was visible. Creepy? It gets better.

We stayed there for awhile taking more pictures and getting readings in earnest. We waited for a long time for something to appear, anything. With no more paranormal activity reported, we continued on our trek. Finally, we saw the Light, the one that we had come to see in the first place. It looked like a small white dot far off in the distance toward Sticky Road, and we weren't as impressed with it as we were with the encounter we'd had earlier.

At this point, we were past the fourth trestle and ready to head back. We sent Rose and another team member ahead on the return trip to see if she could pick up any spirit activity. They had radios, as we all do, and it wasn't long before the radios came to life. Rose reported she was having trouble breathing, and the entire group caught up with her quickly and could see she was experiencing some discomfort. The team member with her was experiencing a choking sensation and rubbing his throat. We realized we were in the same spot as before, when we encountered the figure crossing the tracks. The choking feeling passed, and Rose reported that there were a total of seven spirits in the woods around us. We took more pictures and recordings, then headed to our cars.

We regrouped at a gas station down the road, and discovered some interesting facts. All of the paranormal activity that we recorded had occurred around trestle number three, and we found out that there was a cemetery in the woods close to that area. This could account for the number of spirits encountered. The choking sensation that gripped the two Spirit Seeker members might be explained by a story that I had been told many years ago by my Dad. I had forgotten the story until this incident brought it to mind.

A Rope

My Dad was born and raised in Gurdon. He was the son of a local businessman and saw how hard money was to get in those days. Dad had a

In this photo, we see what appears to be mist forming in front of the investigator. This is sometimes the prelude to a ghostly appearance. Photo courtesy of Spirit Seekers Paranormal Investigation Research and Intervention Team (SPIRIT).

unique way of earning money; he would search the roadways and railways for items he could sell. In turn, he would buy shells for his gun, then hunt in order to provide meat for the table. Dad collected bottles, scraps of steel, or pieces of rope that could be turned into cash at the local junk dealer. One day, while walking the rails in the same general area as we had been, he came across a rope. It appeared to be a new, whole rope; so, thinking he had hit the jackpot, he started rolling it up. At first the rope was easy to retrieve but then it seemed to get hung up, or was tied to something, and became hard to pull. He put down his end of the rope and went to free the other end. At the other end he found the rope tied around the neck of what appeared to be the ghost of a young black man. Needless to say, Dad didn't finish retrieving the rope, but ran home as fast as he could.

This could be the reason that our two team members felt the tightness around their necks. Perhaps they were feeling the pain of the young man who had been hung from the trestle.

Some Conclusions?

There is more to the Gurdon Light than meets the eye, literally. Nobody knows what the Light actually is, even though many have tried to catch it on film to analyze it. All sorts of tests have been performed in an attempt to debunk the haunting theory. They have all failed. The information that we gathered doesn't help either side of the debate, but adds a whole new slant to the tale. We saw the Light, but we also saw a high level of spirit activity at trestle number three. Are they connected in any way? Or, are they two separate hauntings? You decide and let me know.

On a second visit to the tracks outside of Gurdon, we decided not to go home until we found the Light and determined if it was ghostly or not. We actually walked the entire length of track between Sticky Road in Gurdon and Highway 53. A team member was posted with a radio on Sticky Road where the track crosses, and kept in close contact with the other team members. About halfway between the two points, we saw the Gurdon Light. We continued walking and seeing the Light, which never got any bigger. By keeping in constant contact with our lookout, we started seeing a pattern develop. We realized that the railroad tracks, Sticky Road, and the Interstate all come together at the same point, which was where our lookout was posted. When we called in a sighting, the lookout would report that a northbound car had just crossed on the Interstate. It happened every time we thought we saw the spooky light. This could explain what people are seeing today, but the Interstate is fairly new and the lights were seen as far back as 1931.

One of the local Universities, Henderson State, set up a light spectrum test to see if the Gurdon Light was man-made or not. The test results indicate that the light given off is not, and cannot, be man-made. A geologist from the university did a survey of the area and determined that the rock formations, in conjunction with the steel tracks and electricity, could be causing small electrical discharges into the environment and could be seen as balls of light. Other people have set up tests to look for naturally occurring reasons.

All of these tests may in some way explain the light that appears and disappears about midway between Sticky Road and the Interstate, but it does not explain the psychic choking sensation, or the picture of the beheaded man taken at trestle number three.

To see this one, take I-30 west out of Little Rock for about 77 miles. Take Exit 63 onto AR 53 south. You are almost there, so watch close for a railroad crossing. The first one you come to is the place where you should park. Look down the tracks to the west and watch for the light. This is a challenging trek and a person should be in good health to walk the distance required to see the light. But it is also a must see for the paranormal enthusiast. Don't forget to lock your car.

Hot Springs Airship of 1897

Hot Springs, Arkansas

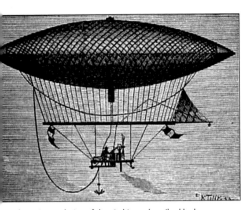

An artist rendering of the airship as described by law enforcement on a dark night in a heavily wooded area near Hot Springs, Arkansas.

One of Arkansas's most enduring legends is that of an airship that mysteriously appeared one night in the Ouachita Mountains. During the period between 1896 and 1897, numerous sightings were reported of men flying around in strange contraptions. Witnesses from California to Alabama, and everywhere in between, were reporting these flying objects to authorities. Though the motorized airship (blimp) would not be invented for several years, people were reporting sightings almost monthly. The operators of the ships sometimes spoke to the witnesses, oftentimes asking them if they wanted to come along on a journey. The mysterious pilots were usually described as tall and dressed in a very strange manner. No one knows who these "people" were, or from where they came. The incident that occurred in Arkansas remains unsolved to this day.

On May 6, 1897, near Hot Springs, Constable John Sumpter and Deputy Sheriff John McLemore were patrolling parts of the Ouachita Forest, looking for cattle rustlers. What they found was something much more sinister and frightening. As the men were riding along the forest trails, they saw what appeared to be an extremely bright light in the night sky. The light faded away and they brushed it aside. Not long after that, the light appeared again, this time settling behind a hill, some distance away. The men pointed their steeds in the direction of the light and went to investigate.

After traveling a little over a mile, the horses stopped and refused to go any further. Something had spooked the animals. The men got down to see what had scared their horses. In the distance, they could see the bright light, this time on the ground, and there seemed to be several individuals moving around it. The men drew their weapons and prepared to investigate the scene.

They approached the strangers, weapons still drawn, and demanded to know their business. A bearded man appeared and informed the two officers that they were traveling through the area and had simply stopped for some water and a short rest.

Sitting behind the man was the strangest looking machine the two lawmen had ever seen. It was fifty to sixty feet long and was shaped like a cigar. The vessel had a large light attached to the front of it. What looked like sails or a gigantic umbrella could be seen through the darkness. The officers noticed another man filling up a container with water, and then they saw a woman. She stood back in the darkness revealing nothing but her silhouette. Strangely enough, she was wearing a dress, hat, and held an umbrella above her head to further hide her from sight.

As the two men stared in bewilderment, the weather was turning and rain had begun to fall. The man with the beard, who was obviously the captain of the strange airship, asked the two men if they would like a ride to a place where it was not raining. The two men declined and stated they "preferred to get wet." The bearded man then commented on how lovely the area was and how he wished he had time to visit the bathhouses in Hot Springs, but he was on a schedule and would have to visit another time.

The two men took their leave, ready to be away from whatever they had come across in those dark woods. After an hour had passed, the men decided to go back and see if the ship was still there. When they arrived at the spot where they had last seen it, it was gone. They never heard the great machine leave and did not see it in the night sky as they rode back to town. Just a few weeks after this incident, a man in Mississippi reported seeing the airship and described it almost exactly as the men in Arkansas had.

Flurry of Reports

The newspapers of the day were filled with accounts of mysterious ships floating through the air. What exactly these people were seeing is unknown. There are many theories as to what was being reported on an almost weekly basis. Some had decided that they were secret projects run by the government; others thought they were visitors from another planet.

What we do know for sure is that one of the first sightings happened in California, in 1896. Nearly 100 people witnessed a large object in the sky; it had an intense light attached to it and seemed to be about 1,000 feet in the air. In the following days and weeks, there were several more sightings from people all over the West Coast.

The flurry of reports started to taper off and people were beginning to forget about the strange objects in the sky when, on February 2, 1897, another ship was spotted near Hastings, Nebraska. This time a farmer claimed he had seen the airship as it was parked near his farm, undergoing repairs. He claimed the object was nearly 200 feet long and 50 feet wide. Leading up to the Arkansas sighting, the ship was seen in Iowa, Illinois, Kansas, Ohio, and several times in and around Chicago.

The sightings usually varied in their descriptions. Sometimes it was longer, sometimes shorter, and some even claimed to have been taken for a short ride with the occupants. However, what is most interesting is that most of the witnesses who had contact with the occupants described them as nervous whenever locals confronted them. To this day, not one person has come forward and stated that they were the original occupants of the airships.

Theories

The theory that these sightings were actually ships from another planet is still hotly debated. The people who put forth this idea point out that motorized airships of the type seen and described by so many people had not been invented yet. Moreover, what about the strange people who were flying these ships? Could it be that they were aliens in disguise? There are many reports of alien encounters where the visitor from another planet would assume the likeness of a human, so as not to frighten those contacted.

We still hear these reports today: "Cigar shaped" is still one of the most used descriptions when eyewitnesses describe a UFO. What if these were visitors from another planet? Would it not make sense that they would try to camouflage themselves and blend in with their environment? These are all legitimate questions.

However, on the other hand, is it not possible that some enterprising people were out there somewhere simply testing out a flying machine that they had invented? The idea of flight was a common one at the time. Airships had been built in small scale for experiments, but it is possible that someone, even several people, had actually perfected the technique needed to fly one of these ships cross country.

When these ships were being seen all over the country, the Wright brothers were only six years away from their famous flight at Kitty Hawk. In their earlier days, even the Wright brothers had experimented with balloons, kites, and all manner of flight-capable objects. Experimenting with these things helped them get the first airplane off the ground on that famous day in 1903.

Around the same time as the sighting in Arkansas, there was a man working on an experimental "flying machine" who lived near Hot Springs. The man had even gone so far as to apply for a patent. The patent application was denied and the man's name has been lost to history, but he did exist. Moreover, if the man was experimenting with some sort of flying machine, he could very well have been one of those unknown culprits that spread so much fear and worry during those two years.

Then there is the story of Charles McDermott, who patented inventions on everything from cotton-picking machines to an "iron wedge." Later dubbed "Flying Charlie," he applied for and received a patent for an "Improvement in Apparatus for Navigating the Air." What he had patented was a flying machine similar to what the Wright brothers had used. It was a machine that was made up of flaps and the operator would lie prone on the machine and operate it with foot pedals. No one can say for certain whether or not McDermott was ever able to get his machines up in the air, but it does add one more possible candidate to the list of those who really were in that ship on that cold and rainy Arkansas night.

What we are left with are numerous questions and not a lot of answers. Any one of the theories about these ships could be true. The sad fact is that we will never know exactly where these airships came from or who was piloting them. For there to be so many sightings of different types of ships seems to rule out that these were just the inventions of creative individuals. It would have taken an enormous amount of wealth to be able to build, test, and eventually fly across the nation in one of these airships.

Arkansas seems to have been somewhat of a magnet for extraterrestrials during that last century and a half. If Arkansas was a frequent spot for those from another planet to visit, would it be entirely out the realm of possibility that these sighting were in fact beings from somewhere else?

Will we ever know exactly what was going on during those two years? Probably not. If it had been one man, or even a small group of men, who were collaborating on the same project, it is more likely than not that someone would have taken credit for the flying ships. The fame and fortune that surely would have been bestowed upon the man or group of men would have been nearly impossible to pass up, even for the most dedicated inventor or scientist.

Until someone finds a definite answer to this mystery, we are left with only our imaginations. Some will believe in the ordinary man who did what, until then, only the birds could do; some will believe that aliens have visited us. Your opinion is no more right or wrong than then next person's. Man has always reached for the stars. That is true today as we send men and women into outer space, and it would have been true all those years ago.

Hot Springs, Arkansas, has been an attraction since early exploration and before. The natural hot water baths have been thought to have magical healing powers and people have gone to Hot Springs to be healed for hundreds of years. To get there, take I-30 west out of Little Rock. Go west for about 28 miles, then merge onto US 70 west via Exit 111. Twenty four more miles on US 70 west and there you are.

Lost Souls

The Rialto Theater
El Dorado, Arkansas

The Rialto Theater in El Dorado is one of the few remaining "movie palace" style theaters left in Arkansas. Notable for its grandeur, size, and Art Deco architecture, the Rialto was added to the National Register of Historic places in 1986. It has a bright and beautiful marquee that hangs out over the sidewalk, enticing the public to come in and sit a spell. One can imagine that, in the not-too-distant past, the sign would boast of air conditioning, and movies like *Gone with the Wind*. If a person were to set their mind to it, they could imagine the teenagers loafing in front of the theater, waiting for a friend, or maybe trying to sneak in the back door for a free movie. Look closer and see a young couple out for a Saturday evening date, and the elderly couple looking to steal some time to rekindle the fire of their younger days.

Some El Dorado History

El Dorado is one of Arkansas's oldest towns, founded in 1843 by a man named Matthew Rainey. Rainey founded the city out of necessity rather than desire. He was passing through, on his way to Texas, when his wagon broke down. He sold all that he owned to tide him over till he could arrange to complete his journey. He was so impressed by the quick sales to the local settlers that he decided to open shop and settle down permanently not far from the Ouachita River. He named the area El Dorado or "The Gilded Road." It was not long after that when El Dorado became the county seat for Union County.

Cotton farming and plantations, along with the lumber industry, helped El Dorado become a thriving community. The area around El Dorado remained a quiet little farming community until the early twentieth century. By then, oil had been discovered and the population was growing out of control. January 10, 1921 is remembered as the date that El Dorado changed from an isolated farming community to the oil capital of Arkansas. Oil was discovered by Sam Busey about a mile south of the town. The boom started and workers descended from every direction. El Dorado went from a population of 4,000 residents to almost 30,000 practically overnight. Neighborhoods of tents were put up to provide housing for the people who came to make their living from oil. Empty lots were filled with makeshift shacks.

Along with the quick growth of tents and shacks came the prosperity to build a rich urban downtown for all to enjoy. Most of the buildings that were built during the boom are still standing today. There are a few buildings built before the boom still standing, but, for the most part, they were not adequate for the large population and were torn down to make more room.

The Railto Theater in El Dorado, Arkansas.

The original site on which The Rialto Theater now stands was the home to a much smaller Rialto that was built in 1921. It was adequate for a city of 4,000, but when the oil boom hit El Dorado, it too was deemed too small to meet the needs of the growing populace. The original theater was torn down, and a new bigger version was constructed in its place.

Verifying Ghosts

The Rialto that is standing today was finished and opened in 1929 at a cost of $250,000. It seated 1,400 people and was home to stage productions, a variety of performances, and movies. A center of entertainment for over seventy years, it closed in 1980. The new owners have vowed to restore the beautiful theater; but first, they want to know if the ghost stories passed down over the years surrounding the old theater are true. The owners contacted a renowned psychic out of Little Rock to walk through the old place. They hoped that she could verify

An investigative photo taken under the marquee. In the upper right, a very bright orb can be seen making its way into the picture. *Photo courtesy of Spirit Seekers Paranormal Investigation Research and Intervention Team (SPIRIT).*

some of the stories, taking into consideration that a psychic can only paint a mental picture of what is happening before them. The owners then allowed me and my team of paranormal investigators to spend the night in the Theater. They wanted more tangible proof that ghosts are lurking in the dark shadows and hiding behind the stage.

We entered the old theater at about eight o'clock in the evening and began setting up equipment and interviewing the owners and some past employees. The owners gave me a tour explaining where it was that they had been told ghosts had been sighted. While talking to past employees and visitors, we found many of them who'd had past encounters that they believed to be supernatural.

One of the employees told me that while he worked in the projection booth, he had seen the door to the booth open and close a couple of times without anyone coming in or going out. There were times when a tool would come up missing only to be found elsewhere in the building or right where it had been left—several days later. These things puzzled the employee, but he admitted that he had never *seen* a ghost. He did say that he never felt like he was alone in the projection booth. Some nights while working late, he would hear people talking outside the booth. When he went out to see who was working late with him, he could not find anyone in the building.

Another former employee said that he used to go backstage to take breaks, and while he was there, he saw something that bothered him. He looked up into the catwalk once and saw what he believed to be a woman climbing the ladder. He did not know why he thought it was a woman, since he could not make out any features or see what kind of clothes the person had on, it was just a feeling. When he called out for this person to come down, she stopped, and then disappeared. That really scared him, thinking that maybe she had fallen. It was so dark that he could not see where she might have gone. He went to the bottom of the ladder, looked around and found nothing.

One patron told me that while he was in the auditorium waiting for the show to start, he noticed a young boy in the curtains by the stage. He said it was like the boy was playing hide and seek, waiting for someone to come find him and peeking out to see if they were coming yet.

Years ago two reporters from a local newspaper set out to spend the night in the theater to see if the stories that they had been hearing were true or not. They believed that there were no such things as ghosts, and were out to prove they were right. They started walking around the old place, using flashlights to guide their way. It was dark, and they started to hear footsteps and knocking from under the stage. The reporters said that these things could be explained away if a person tried, so they did not consider them to be paranormal. Late in the night, they saw some shadows, and they felt cold spots that they could not explain away. However, the one unexplained occurrence that sent them running was when the female reporter felt a hot breath on her neck and heard a whisper in her ear. They left the theater way before sunrise and came back later for their sleeping bags. They still would not admit that they had experienced a supernatural encounter, claiming they had gotten tired and decided to quit early.

While the team was setting up the equipment, our team psychic, Angie, did her walkthrough. When she returned, we set our equipment according to her direction. At this time, I talked with Angie to see what she had found. She told me about an actress who was backstage waiting for the show to start. She said that she got the impression that the actress was there because it was where she belonged and that she had nowhere else to go. Angie also told me about a young boy waiting by the stage. She believed he was a page waiting to seat the visitors and make sure that no one snuck in the back door for free. Angie mentioned that there was a group of teenagers in the back of the theater talking and waiting for one of the group to arrive before settling in to watch the show. She felt like the person they were waiting on was still among the living, but that they are waiting patiently. Two other impressions she talked about were those she received in the balcony. One was of an older man at the projection booth. She felt that he was a handyman waiting to do his job. The other encounter was with an elderly couple sitting and waiting for the show to start. Angie told me that the theater was full of residual energy and lots of happiness. She believed that the spirits were there because it was a place they went to be happy. No negative energy was felt the whole night.

Hotspots

We began our investigation around nine o'clock by sending a team to each hot spot as outlined by the psychic. While walking through the second-floor mezzanine, I smelled a woman's perfume. I set my camera in the vicinity of the washrooms and started recording. While setting up the camera, I heard a very quiet whisper of a female. It sounded like my name being called from a distance. Hopefully, later during our EVP session, we would catch this on recording. Other cameras were set up behind and under the stage, on the stage, in front of the stage, and one in the projection booth. Each camera was operated by an investigator to assure that there were no malfunctions and that each camera had fresh batteries and film. While our static cameras ran, we used handheld digital cameras to take pictures in other areas. This was proving to be an exciting investigation. One of my investigators was grabbed on the ankle while descending the stairs by the second-floor mezzanine. She said that she had been on the third floor and felt like she was being followed. She was on her way to find me to report that she felt like there was an entity by the projection booth. Some of the pictures that had been taken of her as she went down the steps revealed an orb by her feet. Normally, orbs do not get my attention, but when someone feels like they have been grabbed and an orb appears at the same time, I take note of the incident. Other notes of interest involved the sound of doors slamming, music under the stage, and whispered voices from the back corner of the lower seating area.

Evidence Review

After the investigation, we review all potential evidence. During the review, we found what looked like a shadow of a disembodied spirit on the second-floor mezzanine. This coincided with personal encounters of the evening. The door to the projection booth had been left open by the investigator placing the video camera in the room, and the video recorded the booth door closing very slowly and latching. The video camera on the stage was pointing to where the employee had thought he saw a person climb the ladder up the catwalk, above the stage. About forty minutes into the recording, a bright light is seen by the ladder. It appears out of nowhere, remains in front of the camera for about thirty seconds and then disappears slowly. During our EVP session, we recorded several potential disembodied voices. One in particular was especially clear. It was recorded in the back of the theater just as we were preparing to leave. It was in the location where the psychic had told us a group of teens were waiting on a friend. I stated that we were getting ready to leave and wondered if there was someone who would like to say, "Goodbye." The recording, immediately after, caught something that sounded like a sigh, then a couple of words and another sigh. The words were clear enough to say they were words, but not clear enough to tell what was said.

The Rialto Theater is one of my favorites haunts. If you happen to be in El Dorado, stop by and have a look. While you are in the old theater say, "Hi" to the actress under the stage in her dressing room; and whatever you do, do not try to sneak friends in through the back door or the page will have to escort you to the front of the theater and ask you to leave without seeing the rest of the show.

El Dorado is in the extreme southern part of the state. To get there, take I-530 south to Exit 10. At this point take US 167 south to El Dorado. Watch the signs; there are some.

My Honor, My Life

The Dueling Grounds
West Memphis, Arkansas

Code Duello, roughly translated means: "rules of the dueling." In the late 1800s, and for many years before, dueling was the preferred manner in which a man of elite status could regain his honor. Just about any misdeed could trigger a challenge, everything from merely insulting someone to stealing from him. No matter the transgression, the result was the same. The men were joined by their seconds; seconds were men who accompanied the dueler to the dueling field. Each man would have one; they were usually friends of the dueler. The seconds were responsible for loading the pistols and assuring that the duel was fair. Once the pistols had been loaded, the men stood back to back and took roughly ten to twenty paces, turned, and fired. Whoever was left standing was considered the winner.

The duel eventually fell out of favor. As the Civil War dragged on, there were less and less high-class men, who were the principle participants in duels. It had also been deemed illegal, although this never really stopped anyone. The local police often ignored the practice, and went out of their way not to interfere. To do so would have been less than honorable. The last recorded duel in Arkansas took place in 1878, in Pulaski County.

However, there are those who say the duels continue to this day. Deep in the Arkansas brush near the community of West Memphis, out of sight of the living. This place is simply called "The Dueling Grounds." Locals often report strange sounds and lights that originate from this area. Gunshots are commonly heard when you stop and listen quietly to the night. One local resident we spoke to says he has witnessed the ghostly duels.

A Dueling Experience

The year was 1982; Chris Poole and some friends were looking for something to do on a Friday night. They often took their trucks out to the woods, away from parents and police, to drink some beer and hang out. On this particular night, Chris had his high-school sweetheart, Shelly, with him. They had planned to go park, do some drinking, and watch the stars. What they witnessed was something a bit more interesting, says Chris.

He says they were just sitting on the tailgate of his truck, talking, drinking, and having a good time. "I know what you're thinking," he said. "We weren't drunk; we had only been there for half an hour or so." When the cassette tape in the truck reached its end, he went to change it out, and that is when he heard a gunshot quickly followed by another. He did not know if they had stumbled upon poachers or an angry farmer who was trying to warn them off his property.

After wading through the flood waters of the Mississippi River, Alan and Jason found the location of sights and sounds of duels from years gone by.

Chris pulled Shelly into the truck beside him. They sat there and waited for something to happen. Seconds later, another shot rang out, followed by another. The shots echoed through the cab of the truck and Chris decided he wanted to know what they were. Leaving Shelly in the truck, he set off to find the shooters. He had gone about 200 yards or so when he heard several men talking in low voices. Chris eased closer to where the voices were coming from to get a better look.

Standing in a circle were four men. "They didn't look right," Chris said. "They were there, I could see them, but they were sort of transparent." The men were dressed in clothes that were not like anything Chris had ever seen. He described them as looking like they had just stepped off a movie set. As Chris sat there in silence, trying to make sense of what was happening before him, he heard a sound behind him. He turned to see Shelly sneaking up, trying to be quiet. He raised his hands trying to get her to go back, but she kept coming. She nestled down beside him in the weeds and had to stifle a scream when she realized what she was watching.

The four men stood in a circle, two of whom were holding flintlock pistols. They seemed to be in a discussion of some sort, but Chris could not make it out. The man on the left, with a pistol, gestured towards the other armed man, who nodded, and the circle broke apart. The two unarmed men retreated ten to fifteen yards away from the armed men.

Chris was starting to get a clearer picture of what he was witnessing; he had heard the stories of the Dueling Grounds ever since he was a boy. He had always thought they were just stories people made up to keep kids out of the woods. This was no story. Chris realized he was about to witness a duel between two long-dead gentlemen.

The two duelers stood back to back, pistols raised in the air, with bended elbows. The men began to walk away from one another counting aloud as they did 10,9,8,7... When they reached the end of the count, the men turned and pointed their pistols at each other. The man on the right shot first, apparently missing, because the other man laughed and aimed his pistol. As the shot rang out, the second man fell to the ground, obviously wounded. He lay on the ground for several seconds while the other three stared at him.

As suddenly, as he had fallen, the man was being helped up by his ghostly friends. The man checked his vest for holes and brushed himself off before starting to laugh and shake hands with the man who had shot him. They stood around for a few minutes talking, patting each other on the back, and examining their pistols.

Chris turned to Shelly, wide-eyed and asked her if she had just seen what he had seen. She nodded that she had and they both turned back to the apparitions. Chris had been sitting on his haunches for a while and his legs were beginning to ache, so he adjusted his stance; when he did, he stepped on a dry tree branch. It snapped, making a sharp cracking noise. Chris instantly looked towards the men; they were looking his way.

There was no way they could see him, Chris thought. They were well hidden behind trees and underbrush, but the noise had been enough to alarm the men and make them stop their conversation and stare into the brush, ooking for the source of the noise. The man that had been shot walked towards them, pistol in hand. He stopped ten yards from where they were sitting. He stared into the brush for a long time. Chris could not tell if the spirit had seen him or not, until the long-dead dueler smiled, raised his flintlock pistol toward Chris and Shelly and then disappeared. The other men followed suit, and Chris and Shelly found themselves alone in the dark woods trying to understand what they had just seen.

A Soldier Sighting

This would not be the last time ghostly duelers made an appearance. Sometime in the early 1990s, a call came into the Sheriff's Department. The caller stated that he had been out looking over his property when he heard several gunshots. The man refused to give his name, but gave a vague location and hung up the phone.

A deputy was dispatched to the area; he called in that he had arrived at the location and was going to be out of his vehicle while he checked out the report. As soon as he stepped out of the vehicle, he heard the first shot, then the second. He ran towards the direction he thought the shots were coming from, pistol drawn. He quietly searched the woods before finally coming upon his suspects.

What he saw were three men dressed in Confederate uniforms and holding rifles. At first he thought they were just a bunch of drunken reenactors; he would run them off and that would be the end of it. As he stood behind a tree, he took another look at the men before approaching. They were there, but they were not. He could see through them, and they were talking to each other but he could not hear anything. They were silent, even though he could see their lips moving. The men were agitated and seemed to be arguing—over what, he could not tell.

Thinking that his mind was just playing tricks on him, not really believing that he was witnessing spirits, the deputy stepped out from behind the tree and confronted the men. At first, they ignored him. As he yelled at them again to put their guns down, they slowly turned and looked his way. They did not put their guns down. As the moonlight shone upon the men, he could see they were talking again, but as before, no sound came from their lifeless lips. The deputy could see the trees behind them swaying with the wind and realized that he could see the same trees *through* them. The three soldiers were still mouthing to each other as they turned and walked away. When they reached the tree line, they simply disappeared.

Witnesses familiar with this incident verify that a Deputy was called out and that he spent an unusually long period of time out of his cruiser and in the woods, although we could find no official report to verify it.

So, what is really going on out in those woods? Are there spectral visitors from days long past reliving the duels, still trying to save their honor? There are reports that as many as several dozen men lost their lives on these grounds. Perhaps they are getting a second shot at regaining their honor. To this day, reports are made of ghostly encounters with long-dead duelers. Reports of strange lights still persist with no earthly explanations, other than it being the glow of the souls of the men who lost their lives for honor.

Seek if you must; the grounds are not hard to find. There is a sign that marks the spot where so many lost their lives. However, be warned that on certain nights, when the moon is right, you will not be alone in those woods and you might just find yourself on the receiving end of a challenge for your honor, and maybe even your life.

West Memphis is about 130 miles east of Little Rock. To get there take I-40 east out of Little Rock. The dueling grounds are south of town, close to the Mississippi River.

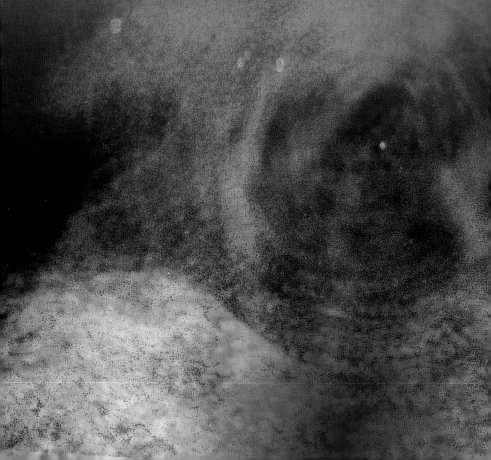

Satan's Corner

Private Residence
Near Russellville, Arkansas

The front porch, just before we entered the house to start the investigation.

A scream in the middle of the night can be very alarming, especially if it is coming from one of your kids' bedrooms. Jeri and Sam, the parents, bolt down the hallway to their son's room to find him standing on his bed crying for an unseen attacker to leave him alone. They grab their son; gather up the other children, and leave the house. What would you do?

Some Historic Background

Satan's Corner, as it has come to be known, is a private residence in Markham, Arkansas. The only thing wrong with this statement is that there is no Markham, Arkansas. The name of the city is a total fabrication made up by a studio producer to hide the true identity of a small city in North Central Arkansas. This story was, and is, so compelling that a mini movie was made about the goings on of the family and their response to the spirit that was found in their home. For the purpose of privacy, this house will be referred to as Satan's Corner, and the location, North Central Arkansas. Our house investigations are kept semi confidential to protect the privacy of the home owner. In this case confidentiality and privacy will be held in high regard but the facts of this haunting will be revealed and the entire family will be telling their stories.

Satan's Corner was built before the Civil War and has been well maintained throughout the years. Very few changes have been made to the structure other than modern utilities brought into the house. The old kitchen still stands in the back of the house and it is now used for storage of lawn-care equipment. There is a cemetery located behind the house that once served as a family plot and then as a place to bury sick or wounded soldiers who had died in the house. The house was used as a hospital during the Civil War. Although no battles are recorded to have taken place in the general area, skirmishes were commonplace. Arkansas had more enemy engagements than any other state during the Civil War. A place for wounded and sick soldiers from both sides was needed and this house was close to well-traveled roads, so it was used as a medical facility.

Paranormal Frights

The current owners of the house had been having problems in the house for some time before they asked for help. The adults, as well as the children, experienced paranormal activity. They were awakened in the middle of the night on many occasions by the sound of voices. It startled them at first, thinking someone had broken into the house. The kids would refuse to go to certain parts of the house alone. They did not sleep in certain rooms. Battery-operated toys operated without being turned on and sometimes the new batteries would drain as soon as the toy was activated. Lights burned out only to be replaced with new bulbs, and they would burn out almost immediately. A plasma mist could be seen in the kitchen from time to time. Everyone in the house felt a presence as if someone were there following them, watching and waiting for them to let down their guard. They were touched by unseen entities, and spirits could be seen moving about in the owner's peripheral vision. The children were being tormented by unseen forces as they slept. We witnessed one such occurrence during our investigation. It was as if the child was having a very bad

The old cemetery behind the house was used as a family plot before the War Between the States. Some of the soldiers treated in the house found their final resting place with the family. *Photo courtesy of Spirit Seekers Paranormal Investigation Research and Intervention Team (SPIRIT).*

dream. Little Nancy was sleeping on a make-shift bed on the floor. As she lay sleeping, she thrashed about and pushed at unseen tormentors.

When we arrived at the house in Markham, we noticed nothing out of the ordinary. The house looked the same as any other old house. It was a nice looking two-story with a big front porch, a homey looking house, one that looked as if anyone was welcome to visit. When we went inside, a very different feeling prevailed. If a person had a smile on their face upon moving through the front door, the smile soon faded. An ominous feeling came over all of us as we entered. It was a feeling of despair, sadness, and sorrow all rolled into one feeling of loss. It was a feeling that existed in every corner of the house.

This feeling that settled on me was not an easy one to explain; it was all of these negative emotions and more. As the night wore on, that feeling never really left us. Nothing was happening in the house, but we all felt like someone was close and ready to spring out at any one of us. At one point, in the evening, one of the investigators went to change out a tape in the upstairs camera and was cast into total darkness as a light failed. When this happened, she screamed as if the devil himself was after her. We had decided early on that no one was to go anywhere alone. She had forgotten the agreement and as soon as she was alone and the lights were out, terror grabbed her mind. It was as if the scream was on her lips waiting to escape at the slightest

A mist of some sort can be seen to the left in this photo. Some people believe that this is a sign of spirit manifestation. *Photo courtesy of Spirit Seekers Paranormal Investigation Research and Intervention Team (SPIRIT).*

excuse. That was how the house made us all feel. It felt like if we were to scream, the tension would be gone.

As the investigation continued into the night, some facts began to be revealed. The house did have several entities in it; one or more of them were not the type one wants to encounter. There are different types of entities that can be encountered while on an investigation. Some spirits existed as humans at one time and may have remained on this level of existence for any number of reasons. These spirits may not know they are dead, or may have unfinished business. These entities are just as they were in life; they may be good, bad, or mischievous, but seldom dangerous. The spirit we do not generally want to meet on an investigation is one that has never been human. If they are causing trouble, they are more likely evil.

The investigators tried various ways of drawing the spirit out of hiding. We finally allowed two of the investigators to try the Talking or Spirit Board. This is not something that we normally condone, but if the circumstances warrant drastic measures, then we do what has to be done. During one session, the planchette was virtually thrown at one of the investigators. One of the questions asked was, "When were you born?" The answer was, "Never." This led investigators to understand that we were dealing with a spirit and not a ghost. Further questioning revealed the name Seth and that he was not there to provide safety, but rather to cause discourse and strife within the family. When asked if he would mind if we did a cleansing, the spirit said that this would not be necessary, that he could handle any unwanted entities. This was a sure fire way of discovering the true reason that Seth was in the house. A good ghost or spirit will not mind a cleansing because they know that it only affects bad or evil energy.

Because of the contact with an evil spirit and the fact that the family was in distress due to the evil spirit, we decided to spiritually cleanse the house. Before starting the cleansing, Angie built a ring of sea salt around the house leaving an opening at the front door. This is done to seal the spirit out once it is removed. Angie and Rose started sageing on the second floor of the house. The entity stayed out in front of them but it was a real battle herding it toward the open door. By the time they had finished the cleansing, they were mentally exhausted. We all sat outside for a short while resting and waiting to see if there would be any repercussions to the cleansing. When we went back inside the house, it held a different feeling. It was peaceful and light. The family was talking and smiling; this was something that we had not seen since we had gotten to the house. The investigators had become energized and ready to talk about the evening. Even though it was very late, the whole house seemed alive and happy. It even appeared that the lights were burning brighter. An evil spirit can be very oppressive to a family and even the house.

Several weeks later, we contacted Jeri and Sam and found out that everything was still good. They said that they had become a close family once again. They all were doing normal family activities instead of hiding in their rooms, wondering what was wrong. They did mention that they had been in close contact with Seth. It appears that he is still around waiting for an opening to reenter their lives. The garage is not connected to their house and it appears that Seth is in there working his evil magic on the car. There are days when the car will not start and there are times when the lights come on by themselves and run down the battery. The trunk lid slammed once barely missing the hands of the lady of the house. But, the house is good and all is well for now.

The Cursed Courthouse

Desha County Courthouse
Arkansas City, Arkansas

The Desha County Courthouse is one of the oldest courthouses still in use. Built in 1900, it is a virtual treasure trove of living history. There are also parts of the courthouse that have nothing to do with the living. There are many spirits said to roam the halls of this building. Some claim former judges and the criminals they presided over walk together in a sort of ghostly truce.

For decades, courthouse workers have experienced all manner of paranormal activity. According to an article in the *Arkansas Democrat-Gazette*, County Assessor Gay Brown reported seeing an apparition one night after working late. Brown claims that, in the early 1990s, she had left the building and gotten into her car. As she turned the key, she looked up at the courthouse and saw a lady standing there in a "white, turn-of-the-century outfit." Brown looked away; when she looked back, the apparition was gone.

The Clock Tower

The strangest story by far concerns the cursed clock tower. According to County Judge Mark McElroy, sometime in the early 1900s, a man stood convicted of arson. The man, known as Jim Williams, nicknamed Willard, had

The old courthouse in Arkansas City. A cold, dismal day greeted investigators as they prepared for the night's investigation.

een gambling in one of the local hotels. As the night wore on, the whiskey flowed like water, and eventually, Willard lost all of his money. Convinced that he had been cheated, he decided to burn down the hotel in retaliation, according to prosecutors. The blaze took hold and burned down several other adjacent buildings as well.

The trial was short, and some say unjust, and Willard was sentenced to hang for his crimes, all the while proclaiming his innocence. Right up until the hangman's noose was around his neck, he claimed he had not set the fire. Then he told a shocked gathering of local residents, who had turned out to watch the hanging that he cursed the courthouse. Specifically, he cursed the clock tower atop the courthouse, saying that it would never tell true time again. Some bystanders claimed that at the moment of Willard's death, the clock stopped.

According to Judge McElroy, the clock has not worked right in the 110 years since Willard's execution. The clock often rings at odd times. On one such occurrence, the bells rang for several hours one night, keeping half the town from getting any sleep. Eventually, McElroy had to get up in the middle of the night and go down to the courthouse. He climbed up into the tower and cut the power to the chimes. Sometimes the hour hands are reversed with the short hand reading the hours and the long hand reading the minutes. The clock has been known to jump ahead and fall behind all in the same day, all without any explanation.

The county soon grew tiresome of the misbehaving clock and called in a clock technician from Florida to fix it. The man arrived, removed the clock from the tower, and took it back to Florida where it was completely restored to its original glory. Weeks later, the clock was reinstalled in the tower. The cursed clock, new parts and all, still refused to run true.

McElroy grew impatient with the clock and tried to come up with a way to reverse the curse on the clock tower. He almost went as far as to hold a mock trial and declare Willard innocent of all charges. Instead, he chose to contact a paranormal group to help him find out for sure whether the courthouse was haunted or just old and problematic. In February of 2009, Judge McElroy chose Spirit Seekers to investigate the old courthouse and look for answers.

The Investigation

The team arrived at 6 p.m. with a team of eight investigators. The team immediately began wiring the building for infrared cameras and audio recording devices. The team deployed one camera in the clock tower itself in hopes of catching any activity that surrounded the clock. Team members then went through the building taking EMF and temperature readings so they would have a baseline reading to compare against any spikes in the data that might occur.

A team psychic was sent in to the building alone to see if she sensed anything out of the ordinary. She immediately felt an overwhelming sense of sadness in the main courtroom area. She then encountered the spirit of an elderly woman who was in the public seating area of the courtroom. The woman was confused and wanted

An investigative photo taken while recording voices in the courtroom. Notice the bright orb in motion. The other orbs are simply dust particles. *Photo courtesy of Spirit Seekers Paranormal Investigation Research and Intervention Team (SPIRIT).*

to know why we were in her courtroom. It was apparent to the psychic that the woman did not realize she had passed on. This situation is more common than one would think. Spirit Seekers has come across this during investigations many times before. It most often happens to those who died unexpectedly, or with great sorrow. The spirit of the woman broke off contact, obviously not wanting to communicate with the psychic any further.

As often happens in a location that has a great deal of paranormal activity, many investigators reported the feeling of being watched as they moved throughout the courthouse. Some investigators also claimed to smell cigar smoke wafting through the air. No one was smoking cigars in or around the courthouse that night. Odd smells are sometimes the result of residual energy that is left in a certain place. Think of it as a VCR replaying a tape repeatedly. The energy from the past does not dissipate, so it is on a sort of loop through time and it just keeps replaying itself.

One of the best pieces of evidence caught that night was captured on one of the video cameras that had been set up in the first-floor hallway. No one was present on this floor, but you can hear a team of investigators coming down the stairs. In the middle of the talking and footsteps of the investigators, something gets right next to the microphone on the camera and lets out a loud sigh. Nothing is seen in the frame of the video, but it seems a spirit was reacting to the fact that investigators were coming back downstairs and it was not happy about it.

The team also captured several EVPs that night. Alan Lowe was in the upstairs courtroom alone with his voice recorder on and recording as he

This picture was taken from outside the window of the Judge's secretary's office. Small and difficult to see, the shadow of a human form can be seen standing in the doorway. The building was empty at the time this photo was taken. *Photo courtesy of Spirit Seekers Paranormal Investigation Research and Intervention Team (SPIRIT).*

asked questions. He asked that if there were any spirits in the room with him, would they please make a noise. A few seconds of silence and then a noise that sounded like footsteps was heard. The footsteps came closer and closer, as if whatever was walking around was coming toward Alan as he spoke.

An investigator using both a voice recorder and an EMF detector, trying to make contact with any spirits in the room, caught the second EVP of the night. An EMF meter records changes in natural and man-made electromagnetic fields; these are fields that are given off by electricity or natural energy. The meter the investigator was using this night had lights that would illuminate as it detected any change in the field. One theory is that spirits may use the surrounding energy to help them manifest, or move objects and make noise. The investigator asked if there were any spirits present that would like to talk with him. After several minutes with no response, he turned on the EMF detector and asked any spirit that might be with them to make the device beep. Seconds later the EMF detector beeped once and only once.

The EVP evidence on this night just kept coming. While I was sitting in the courtroom recording audio and asking questions, I asked if there was anyone in the room with me. I asked that if there was someone there could they please make a noise. Almost immediately, there was a loud bang off to my right. It sounded like someone or something had stomped their foot down hard on the hardwood floor. There were no other investigators on the floor with me, but it was obvious I was not alone.

The final and most interesting EVP captured was also recorded in the courtroom. This seemed to be the hotspot for activity on this night. As the team was gathering its gear and putting things away, preparing to end the investigation, Alan left a recorder sitting in the courtroom while we packed up. Everyone was downstairs helping when the recording was captured. In the main courtroom, a small wooden rail divides the room. In the front of the room is the judge's chair, the jury box, and a desk for the court reporter. On the other side of the railing are the benches for the public to sit on while observing trials and proceedings. In the middle of the rail, there are two small, swinging doors, sort of like those in an old saloon; only these were only about three feet tall. The recording picks up nearly thirty minutes of silence, no talking, and no footsteps. Then out of nowhere, the sound of the swinging doors is heard opening and then swinging shut. There were no living beings in the courtroom when this was recorded.

The Final Verdict

The most convincing piece of evidence obtained that night to prove that the courthouse was indeed haunted came in the form of a single photograph towards the end of the investigation. The photo was taken outside the courthouse looking into the window of the judge's secretary's office. The large windows reveal the shape of a shadow person in the doorway. The shadow form seems to be exiting the room. No discernable human features can be found. The shape is as dark as oil. The office is well lit and any human who would have been in the office at the time the photo was taken would have been easily recognizable. This a very compelling piece of evidence and in the opinion of Spirit Seekers, there is no doubt that the Desha County Courthouse is haunted.

If you are ever in the southern part of the state, near Arkansas City, you should drop by and visit the courthouse. Pack up a picnic basket, sit on the courthouse lawn, and watch the clock. You may just see Willard playing with the hands of time.

This is a beautiful old courthouse in southeast Arkansas on the Arkansas River. To get there, take I-530 south for about 46 miles, then merge onto AR 65 south. Follow that road for about 58 miles and turn east on AR 4. That will get you to Arkansas City. The courthouse is the biggest building in town. While you are there, don't miss the museum that is located across the street.

Mad Max

Sidetracks Pub
North Little Rock,
Arkansas

Sidetracks Pub is a small hole-in-the wall place located in the old part of North Little Rock, the Argenta District. That fact alone makes it most appealing to work-weary patrons. It is the dim lighting and soft music that is so relaxing. A person can enjoy their spirits of choice while watching for the ghost of Anastasia a young prostitute, or maybe the ghost of Maxwell, her would-be lover. Anyway you look at it, the place is loaded with spirits.

The street in front of Sidetracks, which can be seen on the left.

The building in which Sidetracks resides was the last to be built on the block in 1920, as two separate buildings, joined in the middle by a covered walkway. On the north side of the walkway was a brothel owned and operated by Miss Birdie. To the south of the walkway was a bar. The two buildings existing in such close proximity added to their popularity...and violence. Miss Birdie made it very clear that when a person visited her establishment to spend time with one of her girls it was on a first-come, first-served basis. She did not take reservations. But one of the brothel's regulars, a man named Maxwell, took a liking to a young 13-year-old prostitute named Anastasia. Anastasia was very popular with all of the men who frequented Miss Birdies. Maxwell felt that she was his girl and that no one else could see her, ever. This very rough-and-tumble man was kind and gentle to the young prostitute, and brought her special gifts when he came calling at Miss Birdie's. She, on the other hand, took his gifts but played it real cool. She did not want to alienate any of her other customers, and if Miss Birdie caught her playing favorites with any of the customers, she could lose her job.

Late one evening, Maxwell was sitting in the bar when another man came in and started bragging about his visit to Miss Birdie's. The drunken barge worker boasted about seeing a young girl named Anastasia. Maxwell had been drinking hard and became very angry at the man. The man started laughing at him and a brief fight ensued. Maxwell broke loose and stormed into Miss Birdie's looking for his girl. No one could stop him from bolting upstairs to Anastasia's room. Miss Birdie was in hot pursuit trying to stop him and avert a brawl in her establishment. Back in those days, and particularly in Argenta, the police did not respond to fights in bars or whorehouses.

When he confronted her, she did not deny that she saw other men. Maxwell's anger was uncontrollable at this point. He drew a knife from his boot and waved it in front of her face. Miss Birdie backed off, and Maxwell grabbed Anastasia by the back of the head. With his fingers entwined in her hair, he pulled her head back and slit her throat. He cut her so deeply that only the spinal column held her head in place. He threw her bleeding body out of the window and jumped after her, escaping for the time being.

The brutal murder of Anastasia had far-reaching ramifications. It ultimately caused the brothel to be closed, and authorities were forced to keep a watchful eye on the bar that so many rough men visited while docked at ports along the river.

The covered walkway that once separated the bar and the brothel was removed and a wall was built to divide the two buildings. The bar remained open, but the rowdies were replaced with a more quiet clientele. In 1923, a mortuary moved into the old brothel. Business was good for the mortuary. The only problem was that the funeral home was across the street, and hauling the bodies out of the building and crossing the street was not a pleasant sight for the town people. The citizens began to complain about the unacceptable conditions that existed in the downtown buildings. They felt that if Argenta was to ever hope to become a real city, the fights, murders and the carting of the city's dead across Main Street would have to end. So, a basement was built in the mortuary and a tunnel connecting it to the funeral home was dug. Now, the bodies could be transported to the funeral home without public knowledge. Still, this was not the best situation, so the mortuary was eventually moved to the backside of the funeral home, and the old brothel was once again empty.

Main Street was growing, and Argenta was finally incorporated. The city leaders vowed to clean up Main Street. The funeral home eventually closed,

An investigative photo taken inside the bar. The steps are where the prostitute and her lover fought, and she met her death at the top when her throat was cut. *Photo courtesy of Spirit Seekers Paranormal Investigation Research and Intervention Team (SPIRIT).*

and the connecting tunnel and basement of the old brothel were filled in. Workers told anyone who would listen that when they filled in the basement, they covered up old mortuary equipment, and even some unclaimed bodies that had been left behind when the funeral home closed the tunnel.

In 1929, a newspaper stand opened in the building. The news stand was just a front for the sale of illegal alcohol to anybody who had the money to buy it. Our old buddy Maxwell made a re-appearance at this time and met some of his old friends. One of the patrons remembered him as the man who'd killed a little girl named Anastasia a few years earlier in that very building. He confronted Maxwell, and a fight between the two ensued. Maxwell did not have a chance, and was stabbed to death.

In 1935, the two buildings were merged into one by breaking passageways through the brick wall that divided them. Maxwell's Coffee House was established and opened to the public. The name was deceptive in that liquor was still the main beverage sold to an all-male clientele. They did sell some food to stay straight with the law. By the '40s, the one time bar/brothel was sold again. This time the new owners catered to men and women. The name of the joint was still Maxwell's Coffee House, and fights were still commonplace.

Time mellowed the wild town of Argenta and the name changed to North Little Rock. The building closed and fell into disrepair. By 1996, it was bought once again and renamed Diamond Jim's Fine Dining. The building was restored with the addition of chandeliers and polished brass trim everywhere.

Strange Happenings

It was about this time in the building's history that strange happenings started. The construction workers had to stop work regularly because of missing tools or unplugged equipment. After restoration, the new owners had similar experiences. They had water faucets that turned on and off without human assistance. They had lights that dimmed and brightened, drawers that opened and closed, and a stove that lit itself. Things happened so often that they had trouble keeping employees.

Nowadays, the strange occurrences aren't limited to just the staff; patrons get to enjoy an evening watching things move across the bar or jump into the air. These things and more are why a team of investigators from Spirit Seekers was asked to come spend the night at Sidetracks.

The excitement started soon after the investigation began. Our psychic was at the top of the stairs when she felt the presence of a young female. She picked up a name that sounded like "Stascia" or "Anastasia." The feeling was so strong that we all gathered to start taking readings. The EMF meter was bouncing off the charts and the temperature readings were moving up and down the scale so much so that it was hard to keep up with. We were definitely in the presence of an entity. The readings came to a sudden stop for unknown reasons, but as one of our skeptical investigators was coming to the top of the stairs to see what was going on, he felt something brush by, then felt a grip on his shoulder. He said it felt like someone had grabbed him. It made him turn to see who was coming up behind him but no one was even close. The closest was an investigator named Sam and she was at the bottom of the stairs. She, too, was involved with the entity. She was waiting at the foot of the steps and soon she felt a cold grip on her arm followed by a gentle caress as if to say, "Sorry if I squeezed too hard."

Later that night, we ran into a spirit that became know to us as Len. The psychic felt that this was either a last name or a nick name. Could this have been Maxwell's last name? She said he wasn't happy and wanted us to leave. The area in front of the bar became oppressive and heavy feeling. It felt as if a real negative, unhappy person had walked into the room. Our equipment was not indicating a spirit presence, but none of us wanted to stay there long enough to really give it a chance to work. After the investigation, the owners of the bar showed us a picture they had taken not long before we came to the establishment to conduct the investigation. The picture is of the bar and some of their patrons enjoying the nightlife; but if you look at the mirror behind them, you can see a face of a man scowling as if he were mad at the world. This man was not in the group and did not work at the bar. Matter of fact, the man in the picture did not have a body; a head was all that was visible. This picture is what compelled the owners to call Spirit Seekers.

A night a Sidetracks Pub will provide more spirits than you pay for, and if you're lucky, you can meet Anastasia or Maxwell. Just don't get between them, or Max might get mad and who knows what will happen.

Sidetracks Pub is located at 415 Main Street in the Argenta District of North Little Rock.

White River Monster

Newport, Arkansas

Deep in the waters of the White River, near Newport, Arkansas, swims a monster. The cryptid creature has been sighted sporadically since the 1800s. Tales of water-bound monsters are nothing new. Most of us have heard the tale of the Loch Ness Monster. Like its Scottish cousin, the White River Monster is adept at avoiding detection and capture.

The first sighting on record is the tale told by a young Indian brave. Although mystic creatures and legends are common in many, if not all Native American cultures, they are not usually cast down and picked up through the years by the mainstream population.

The White River near where the search was conducted for the river monster

A large, barren island that would sporadically appear within the river… One intrepid brave stepped atop the fleshy mound and suddenly spotted a large, ponderous head rising up from the land mass. Frightened, the brave leapt into his canoe and paddled toward shore, but the thrashing monster overturned his little boat. The brave barely survived, and the "island'" sank into the depths.

This is the first sighting of what has been dubbed "The White River Monster" or "Whitey," as it was later named. The re-telling of this account first

The White River Monster gained national attention, and professionals were brought in to help find and remove the monster, or help disprove its existence. According to locals, "Whitie" can be seen today swimming in the waters close to Jacksonport, Arkansas. *Photo and caption courtesy of Popular Science Magazine, circa 1937.*

appeared in *The Field Guide to North American Monsters* by W. Haden Blackman. This incident is believed to have occurred in the early 1800s; an exact date is unknown. Although this is the first documented sighting, it was not until 1937 that Whitey made national headlines.

Before we get to the most famous headlines about the monster, it is important to note that two sightings superseded the circus that surrounded the 1937 sighting. In 1915, Newport resident George Mann witnessed the first appearance of Whitey in the twentieth century. Although there is no record of a formal report, Mann claimed to friends and family to have seen the monster. The second sighting occurred on July 9, 1924. Little Rock native Mrs. Ethel Smith claimed she nearly came face to face with the creature.

> The thing stayed on top of the water about five or ten minutes. It was making a terrible blowing noise, but never did show its head or tail. It was a terrible-looking thing with dingy, gray crusted hide.

See the Monster Here

The authorities took neither of these two claims seriously. The reports were eventually forgotten, with the exception of being good campfire stories to scare the kiddies.

Then just thirteen short years later, On July 1, 1937, Bramlett Bateman, a local plantation owner, was summoned to the river's edge by sharecropper, Dee Wyatt. The man claimed he and his wife had seen "a monster" just off the banks of the White River. Bateman was understandably skeptical of the claim, but reluctantly he peered over the land's edge and, undoubtedly to his surprise, there was the monster. He let out an audible cry and immediately took off toward Newport, some six miles away, to report what he had seen.

Bateman reported the monster to be "as big as a box car and as slick as a slimy elephant without legs." The first person he contacted was D.N. Graves of the Arkansas Game and Fish Commission. He wanted Graves to give him permission to dynamite the area where he had seen the monster. This request was dismissed on the grounds that it was illegal to blast in an inland waterway. The only exception was when the dead body of a drowning victim needed to be dislodged from the river bottom. It is permissible to blast for bodies but not for monsters. Word soon spread of Bateman's sighting, and by July 8th, Bateman's farm had turned into a tourist attraction.

At first, it seems the monster sightings arrived as common sense left the area. Bateman and the Newport Chamber of Commerce created a "see the monster here" viewing site, complete with a fence and twenty-five-cent admission price. As hundreds crowded the small area, Bateman, being the ever-industrious entrepreneur, began selling sandwiches and cold drinks to the public. One overzealous patron showed up with a fully automatic Tommy gun, just in case the monster decided to attack the boisterous crowd. It was an event that could not be missed. Fathers brought their children; old men brought their wives, all hoping for just a glimpse of the creature.

The next few days saw a flurry of activity. Deputy Sheriff Z.B. Reid claimed he saw the monster for just a few seconds and opined that it looked like an extra-large Catfish. Reid said he only saw the back rising out of the water, but that its back was at least 10 feet in length. There were no shortages of theories as to what was being seen by so many. Some guessed that it was an inverted, capsized boat that was rising and falling with the tides. Others surmised it could be a large sturgeon or even a wayward deep-sea animal that had made its way up the Mississippi river and down into the tributaries.

In addition to Reid, two other local residents signed affidavits, claiming they had also seen the monster. It turns out these two, Mrs. Bateman, and J.M. Gawf never actually saw the body of the monster, only strange ripples in the water. They assumed these ripples had to be caused by the monster—caught up in the moment, in their minds, what else could it have been?

The madness of the event continued, and on July 12th, a local man, W.E. Penix announced he was going to construct a large rope net with which to catch the sea-monster. Penix claimed he would have the net ready the following week and would be accepting donations to help cover the costs. He also planned to have a local radio station broadcast live and on location when the capture was made. Soon after making his dramatic intentions known, Penix announced he was giving up on his attempt to capture the monster. It seems donations had dried up and he had no supplies with which to construct his monster-net. The radio station ultimately backed out of the deal as well, citing a lack of profitability in the endeavor.

A short time later, the Newport Chamber of Commerce announced it had retained the services of Charles B. Brown, an ex-military diver based out of Memphis. They announced that Brown would conduct his underwater monster hunt beginning on July 22nd and ending three days later. People from all over the country came to witness the dive. Newspaper reporters arrived in droves, eager to break the story when Brown finally encountered the monster.

The first day of the scheduled dive was a holiday in the town of Newport. Stores closed, nobody went to work, farmers did not farm, and housewives did no housework. The entire community—which by that point had grown by several hundred souls in the past few days—had nothing on their collective minds save for one brave diver and a monster they all wanted to see for themselves.

The moment everyone had been anticipating finally arrived. Brown, outfitted in his diving gear, emerged ready for battle. In addition to his diving apparatus, he donned a razor sharp, several foot-long whale harpoon. He must have truly appeared ready for a fight to the end; unfortunately, the only enemy he confronted on his first day was the muddy silt of the White River. Visibility was only a few inches and Brown emerged from the mud and muck less than two hours after he had descended, empty-handed with no monster slung over his shoulder. Later that afternoon, he submerged himself again. By the time he had resurfaced, a large portion of the crowd had dissipated, succumbing to boredom. Most made their way to local taverns or outdoor celebrations in honor of the event. They danced, drank, and shared stories and bits of gossip they had picked up.

The following day, Brown tried again, albeit for a much smaller crowd. An air valve malfunctioned on his helmet and Brown was forced to stop for the day after only a short time in the water and no sighting of the monster he had come to conquer. There are no reports that Brown even attempted to dive on what was to be the third and final day of the excursion. Eventually, the area returned to normal, sightings tapered off, and soon, "The White River Monster" was only a fading memory. A couple of sporadic reports were filed through the years, but none was seriously investigated.

New Sightings

Then, in June of 1971, the monster was back. Earnest Denks reported he had seen the long absent monster.

It was gray, real long, pointy bone protruding from its forehead. It looked as if it could eat anything, anywhere, anytime.

The sightings did not stop there; on June 28th, Cloyce Warren was fishing with some friends near Newport when they spotted the monster.

This giant form rose to the surface and began moving in the middle of the river away from the boat. It was very long and gray colored. We had taken a little Polaroid Swinger with us to take pictures of the fish we caught. I grabbed the camera and managed to get a picture right before it submerged. It appeared to have a spiny backbone that stretched for 30 feet or more…

In all, there were seven sightings in 1971. In July of that year, Sheriff Ralph Henderson of Jackson County found two trails of suspicious footprints. The first trail lead away from the river's edge, ripping up vegetation as it went. The second set of tracks lead back into the river, just a few feet from the outbound tracks. Plaster casts were made of the tracks and are, "fourteen inches long, eight inches wide, three-toed claws with a spur extending at an angle from the heel."

That is all it took for the media spotlight to be cast upon the area once again. The news spread even quicker than it did for the 1937 sighting. It literally went around the world. Scores of statewide media descended upon the small town of Newport and Jacksonport. Even CBS news dispatched crews with hopes of catching a glimpse of the illusive creature. A Japanese filmmaker was among the throngs of hopeful witnesses. It did not take long for the local businesses to realize they had a "cash monster" on their hands. You could buy hats, t-shirts, postcards, and you could sit down to enjoy a mouth-watering "Monsterburger" at a local diner. Even Folksinger Jimmy Driftwood threw his hat into the ring, penning a song about the monster.

What Is It?

The debate as to what "The White River Monster" really is still goes on. There are plenty of ideas and conjecture, but not one person has been able to come up with an absolute explanation for the sightings. The guesses run the gamut, from a large alligator or a giant catfish, to an oversized gar. The Warren photograph taken in 1971 leaves much to the imagination. It is a grainy somewhat out-of-focus shot. It shows what appears to be something floating in the water, but it is by no means absolute evidence of a monster. It could just as easily be a floating log.

The only semi-plausible explanation is from Roy P. Mackal, a cryptozoologist, in his book, *Searching for Hidden Animals*. He concludes that the monster fits the characteristics of a "Mirounga angustirostris," otherwise known as the elephant seal. The color, size, and shape all fit the varying descriptions given by eyewitnesses over the years. Mackal claims that an elephant seal could easily have made its way up from the Gulf of Mexico into tributaries, then into the Mississippi, and eventually, into the White River. However, as pointed out by several experts, the "Mirounga angustirostris" is primarily found near Baja, California and the western coast of Mexico. That means for this animal to even make it to the Gulf of Mexico, where it could work its way up to the White River, it would have to pass through the Panama Canal, a very unlikely scenario at best.

In addition, Mackal's theory does not explain how the creature has been seen at varying times over the last 150 years. The legend of the monster goes back to the Quapaw Indians. Surely, one elephant seal could not have a life span of 150 years at a minimum. Are we to believe that several elephant seals have made their way to the White River? Not only is that highly unlikely, the odds of that happening are surely astronomical.

So we ask: What is the White River Monster? Is it really a monster at all or just a wayward elephant seal? Another explanation that has garnered some attention is that it is just a giant catfish. The stories of giant catfish are plentiful in and around Arkansas. Try doing a search on the Internet; what comes up is a plethora of pictures of men standing next to six- and ten-foot-long catfish. Could there really have been a fish out there that was big enough for a small Indian boy to actually step out of his canoe and onto the top of it? Then there is the matter of the horn-like structure protruding out of the head. Have you ever seen a freshwater fish with a horn? Some of the reported sightings have the monster making an awful noise, like a cow in pain. I have never heard a fish bellow, much less sound like cow.

Ultimately, it is you, the reader, who must decide what to believe. It is important to note that it is impossible to prove something does not exist, only that it has not been found thus far. You may even want to travel to Jacksonport or Newport to take in a little fishing and sightseeing. Be warned: If do you encounter "The White River Monster," you would be advised to slowly row your boat away from the creature, lest you violate Arkansas state law. In 1973, Senator Robert Harvey of Swifton introduced a bill to protect the monster. The bill passed by voice vote, creating the White River Monster Refuge, making it illegal to "molest, kill, trample or harm the White River Monster while he is in retreat."

Hope is not lost, you can see the monster every Christmas in Newport he is the featured float in the annual parade. Grab a t-shirt and a hat and you can tell everyone you saw the White River Monster while eating a corndog and lived to tell about it in Newport, Arkansas.

To find Newport, take US 67 north out of Little Rock. Take US 67 north about 84 miles to Exit 82. At Exit 82, merge onto AR 17 toward Newport. Finish up your trip by going another three miles into Newport. Remember the White River Monster is protected by state law.

Get Out

McCollum/Chidester House
Camden, Arkansas

The beautiful old frontier home built by Peter McCollum, in 1847, was located on the western outskirts of town. The location made it very desirable to the next owner, since it was situated close to the well-traveled trade route that wound its way to Washington, Arkansas. McCollum had comfort in mind when he built the house, which he outfitted with many eastern imports. The kitchen had an iron cook stove and all of the necessary amenities to make it top of the line. Other items that made the McCollum house special were carpeted floors and plastered walls, as well as the seven rooms downstairs and three upstairs, with five fireplaces. Peter McCollum lived in the house for fifteen years before moving to a larger place further west of town. It was sold to an entrepreneur by the name of John Chidester in 1858.

Chidester was a hardworking government contract mail carrier, who had operated stage lines in several other states before coming to Arkansas. As the railroad moved closer to him, he would move farther west in an attempt to stay ahead of them. Eventually, the railroads caused the stagecoach to no longer be a viable means of transportation. When John Chidester bought the house, he bought it to serve as a home for his family and a layover for his stagecoach. As business grew, so did the house and outlying support buildings. He added two more rooms to the already large house, as he needed room for both his family and his stagecoach drivers. The upper two rooms were reserved for the drivers. The stagecoach business was booming and Camden was growing. As many as twenty passengers came to Camden via stagecoach each day and places to stay were needed. Three hotels were built to accommodate the influx of visitors: The Commercial Hotel, the Southland House, and the Ouachita House—all cared for the travelers in grand style.

As the Civil War approached, stagecoach business in Arkansas began to decline. The mail contracts were being reevaluated and people were afraid to travel. Once Arkansas seceded from the union, virtually all mail to the southern states stopped flowing through regular channels. John Chidester became involved with the southern Confederacy by helping supply letters containing valuable information concerning Union troop movements. He continued to aid the Confederacy in this manor until Union General Fredrick Steele came to Camden with his army. He made his headquarters at the Chidester House and fully intended to arrest Mr. Chidester as a spy for aiding and abetting the Confederates in their attempt to overthrow the US government. Chidester evaded the Union troops by hiding in a small secret room in the house until they stopped looking for him. He then quietly left the house and headed for Texas, where he remained for the remainder of

The McCollum/Chidester House in Camden, Arkansas.

the war. After the war, he was granted amnesty for his crimes against the United States and came back to Camden to reopen his stage line. He stayed in business until 1881, when the railroad finally arrived to take the place of stagecoach traffic.

Special Guests

The Chidester Family retained ownership of the house until 1963 when they sold it to the Ouachita County Historical Society. It is currently a museum and is open to the public most of the year. Throughout the house, original furniture, clothing, and day-to-day comforts can be seen by visitors. Most of the furnishings are original to the house and the Chidester family.

Other original items that came with the house are the disembodied spirits roaming from room to room. Some believe that they are the spirits of family who refuse to move on. There have been so many stories told about ghostly apparitions in and around the house, that I was contacted by The Ouachita County Historical Society to come and check out the late-night visitors at the McCollum Chidester House.

Over the years, stories of ghostly encounters at the old Chidester House have been told and retold, giving the old house an eerie reputation of being haunted. The Ouachita County Historical Society obtained the house in 1963, and soon after started to notice various indicators that the old house might be haunted. Like many other people, they were hesitant to share their stories with the other members for fear they might be thought slightly off kilter. This is a common occurrence when the living first meet the spirit world.

One female member of the society was in the back kitchen area of the house cleaning up when she caught an unidentified aroma, and stopped cleaning to investigate the smell. The smell went as quickly as it had come and she could not trace it. Soon after returning to work, the smell came again, and this time she was able to identify it as freshly baked bread. She tried to locate the smell by walking around the house, but every time she left the room, the smell disappeared. She thought that maybe someone near the house was baking bread, so she went outside and walked around the house. The smell was not outside. Inside, the aroma of the freshly baked bread was stronger now, and only in the kitchen area. The smell did not frighten her, but made her feel more at home. It brought back long lost memories and made her days at work seem more bearable. When her husband returned to pick her up, he commented on the smell of bread baking. They both checked the house again and made sure the oven was not on before leaving for the day.

One afternoon, a former staff person was working on the far side of the house putting displays in order. She heard footsteps coming toward her. They were heavy footsteps that sounded like a man's boot-clad feet. She knew that one of her fellow workers wore heavy boots and thought it might be him, but when she called his name, she received no response. This made her wonder if someone she did not know had come into the house, so she went to check. She found everything just as she had left it, and the doors were all closed and secured from the inside. This was a little unnerving, so she turned out the lights and left the house as quickly as she could.

Most recently, some of the staff experienced feelings of not being alone. They have been touched, felt cold spots in the heat of summer, heard whispers from rooms that were empty, had things moved only to turn up days later, and they have seen mysterious manifestations in the house.

One staff member told me he was working in one of the bedrooms and looked up to see a blue mist forming in the parlor. This concerned him somewhat because he thought it might be smoke, and in an old house like the Chidester, that can be a very scary possibility. As he approached the blue mist, it began to dissipate, and by the time he reached the parlor, it was gone. There was no lingering mist or smell of any kind. Could this have been one of the Chidesters trying to make themselves known to him?

The same staff person had a picture taken a few years earlier in the back room that joined the kitchen, as though the photographer stepped in the back door and snapped the inside of the room. A mirror was on the opposite wall and caught the reflection of a man in a three-piece suit. This guest thought she was alone at the time, but it is very clear that she had an unexpected visitor with her.

Proving a Haunting

I was given the rare opportunity to come to the old house to look for proof of a haunting or provide rational explanations for the activity that the staff was experiencing. I took a small group of investigators to the house one cold November night. We had not been in the house long when my investigators started having supernatural encounters. One team member had been upstairs in a bedroom when he heard someone say the word "hiding." It confused him, in that he could not figure out what significance the word "hiding" would have. We noted it, and continued the investigation.

Soon another investigator had both a male and female spirit communicating with her. They were both telling her "steel" or "steal," and she could not be sure which it was. Often, during an investigation, communicating spirits are only able to divulge one word at a time, and it can be extremely frustrating trying to discern the meaning.

Another female investigator had a feeling that someone had hidden in an upstairs closet; then, still another investigator was pushed while trying to collect electronic voice phenomena. He was trying to go into a small closet in an upstairs bedroom and was physically pushed out. While listening to his audio recording taken during this time, we heard the words, "Get out."

Finally, all of this evidence was presented to a staff member, to see if it made any sense to him. He told us about the time, late in the Civil War, when General Steele came to the house to arrest John Chidester for treason; and Mr. Chidester hid in the upstairs closet to avoid arrest. It made perfect sense at that point. The spirit or spirits were trying to tell us their story in their own words.

Thinking back to some of the stories told to me during the research for this chapter, I can see that the old house is ready to tell its history to anybody who will take the time to listen. The McCollum/Chidester House serves as a

An investigative photo taken in the master bedroom. The black mass is not a shadow of any person in the room. The investigator was alone when he took this picture and the room was totally dark. It is believed to be the photograph of a shadow spirit. *Photo courtesy of Spirit Seekers Paranormal Investigation Research and Intervention Team (SPIRIT).*

museum and is open to the public most of the year. If you choose to visit, open your ears and listen closely. While there, you may get more than a casual tour through the house by a historic guide. If you are lucky, you may get a personal tour from one of the Chidesters. But you might not want to go into the small closet upstairs; it gets a little crowded, and you may be told to get out.

To get to this beautiful old home that is now a museum, take I-530/US 167 south out of Little Rock toward Sheridan. After 55 miles take Exit 10 and merge onto US 167 south. Continue for 29 miles from Sheridan to Camden on US 79. Follow the signs to Camden. The museum is located in the center of town at 926 Washington Street.

Unholy Church

The 1925 First Methodist Church
Smackover, Arkansas

The haunted church in Smackover, Arkansas.

In the small town of Smackover, Arkansas there is a library in the basement of an old Methodist church. What resides in that library is neither from Heaven nor Earth. This is a firsthand account of what happened the night a group from Spirit Seekers Paranormal Investigation Research & Intervention Team conducted a paranormal investigation inside this building.

An Investigation

We arrived at the investigation site about seven p.m.; two investigators and I were the first to enter the building. The library had been converted from a church that was built in 1925. It has two levels. The upper level, which served as the sanctuary when it was still a church is now a meeting place for local groups. The basement portion of the church was converted into a small library to serve the people of Smackover.

Team members Paul and Kim headed downstairs while I stayed on the upper floor to conduct baseline EMF (electromagnetic field) readings. All readings were normal with no spikes; the base temperature was also holding steady with no fluctuations. I began to conduct an EVP session to see if I could pick up anything. (As mentioned before, when conducting an EVP session, investigators use small voice recorders to try and illicit responses to questions asked aloud. The theory is that some spirits can use the energy in the room to give short answers to questions that are later heard when played back.) After about fifteen minutes of asking random questions, I switched the recorder off and made my way downstairs to join the other team members.

Immediately upon descending the staircase, I was overcome with an enveloping feeling of tension and dread. It was all around me. It suddenly became hard to breathe and the air was like a thick, wet, invisible fog. As I stood at the bottom of the staircase, trying to catch my breath, something caught my attention. I am not sure if it was something I heard or saw out of my peripheral vision, but something was "drawing" me to a certain corner at the back of the room. As I headed back to this corner, Paul told me he had been drawn there as well when he first came downstairs.

As I got closer to that corner of the room, the feeling of tension was overwhelming. I was taking quick, shallow breaths as I walked. Every step that took me closer to that part of the room was an act of sheer willpower. I did not want to go, but I felt as if I had to. I felt that if I did not go to it, whatever "it" was, it would come to me. I had no choice. I eased back to the corner, stopped, and looked back to make sure my fellow investigators were still there. I stood there looking and listening for anything that would give me a clue as to what had summoned me.

I stood there for maybe five minutes just breathing in the heavy air and waiting. I am not sure what I was waiting for, but I had expectations of grandeur. Would an apparition suddenly appear and give me all the answers I had been looking for? Would it speak to me? All of these things ran through my mind, but nothing happened. I just stood there feeling as if something was going to come out of the darkness at any second. Nothing did, at least not yet.

The other two investigators and myself decided to conduct an EVP session while having Paul sit in a chair in that particular corner with a video camera filming him. We asked our questions, and as we progressed, Paul began to feel uneasy. The chair was facing an empty row between two bookshelves. Something kept catching his eye, but he could not make out what it was. As he was staring into the darkness, the uneasiness continued. Paul began to feel like it was getting warmer around him and he had an intense nervous feeling, as if something was going to come charging at him out of the darkness. Paul decided he had all the time in the chair that he wanted and asked for someone else to take his place for a while. Reluctantly, I agreed.

Not Alone

As soon as I sat down, I instantly felt it. The temperature seemed as if it were at least 5-10 degrees higher in that corner than it was anywhere else in the room. After only a few minutes of sitting there, I began to get a bit light-headed. Another odd sensation, one that I have never experienced on an investigation before, was pressure in my ears. It felt as if I were on an airplane that was descending. That can mean only one thing: a localized change in barometric pressure. This is important because it is solid evidence that something unusual was going on in that room. The barometric pressure does not just change without reason. Something has to make it change.

I realized that I had been sweating profusely, even though the temperature in the room was never above sixty degrees. Even with the elevated temperature

An investigative photo taken in the lower floor of the old church, where the town library is located. This is the location where the evil spirit manifested to three investigators, at three different times. *Photo courtesy of Spirit Seekers Paranormal Investigation Research and Intervention Team (SPIRIT).*

that I was feeling while sitting in the chair, it was nowhere near warm enough to explain this. I began taking deep breaths to calm myself down. I tried to distract myself by concentrating on the darkness in front of me, between the two bookshelves. That is when I first saw it.

It is hard to describe the feeling one gets when one witnesses something truly supernatural. It is a guttural feeling that slingshots from awe to fear and back again. One runs though an entire gamut of emotions. All at once, I wanted to jump up, point, and scream to my teammates to look and see what I was seeing. On the other hand, I was afraid that if I brought attention to it, it would disappear. I sat there, in the darkness, and witnessed what I had been waiting my entire paranormal career for: the attempted materialization of a full-body apparition. In the paranormal world, this is "The Holy Grail," and there it was, no more than ten feet away. I sat in silence and waited to see what would happen next.

To understand what I witnessed, you would have to imagine yourself in a thick fog bank. That's the way it felt to me. I could see something coming through the fog, and then it would retreat, as if it did not want me to get a clear view of it. I kept staring, my eyes straining to make out a shape in what seemed like a mist. It took almost five minutes before I could actually see the shape of what was appearing in front of me. The shape was that of a human figure. It had not fully materialized, but there was no mistaking what it was.

To understand how significant this is for me, you have to know me. As a paranormal investigator I am a skeptic, some say a doubter who will never fully believe no matter what I witness. I do not believe easily. I often tell people "show me," and when they cannot, I dismiss their story as a misunderstanding or a naturally occurring phenomenon. Oftentimes I am too skeptical. Nothing cures skepticism like an apparition attempting to materialize in front of one's own eyes.

I could not shake the feeling of dread as I watched this "thing" fade in and out. The air was still thick and I was struggling to breathe. In addition, my ears were starting to pop—the air pressure again—it was getting to the point of being slightly painful. I did not blink. I was afraid if I did, the apparition would completely disappear. After about ten minutes, the shape started to dissipate. I could barely make it out at that point, and at the same time, the air around me was returning to normal. It was no longer hard to breathe and the pain in my ears had subsided to a dull throb. A few seconds later, the apparition was completely gone.

I sat there for a few minutes trying to comprehend what I had just been witness to. Eventually, I got up and walked around the room just trying to make sense of it all and trying to calm myself down. I was a bit shaken. Around this time, our lead investigator was arriving and we explained to him what had happened. Understandably, he wanted to try to recreate the experience. I told him I needed to run outside to get some batteries for my equipment and they should start without me. I did not need batteries. I just needed to get out of that place for a while. I think he knew this, and thankfully, did not argue the point. Only later did he tell me that he too saw the shape of a man in the same corner where I had been sitting.

While I sat outside, I thought quite a bit about what I had just experienced. It seemed so surreal; just a few minutes earlier I was witnessing something that was not of this earth and now I was outside breathing in the cool night air and trying to make sense of it all. After about fifteen minutes, I decided to rejoin my team members. I had no idea what I was about to walk into.

Get Out

As I entered the sanctuary of the old church and was about to descend the stairs, Kim came running up and collapsed on the floor. She was crying hysterically, and clutching her chest. She was sitting on her knees, almost in a fetal position. I tried to calm her down and find out what had happened in the short time I had been gone. She would not answer me. She just kept saying she had to get out of this place, so I got her up and she went outside. Alan, the lead investigator, and Paul came up as Kim was going outside. I asked what was happening and they would not tell me anything until everyone was out of the building.

Once outside Alan explained that they had tried to communicate with the "spirit" using dowsing rods. Asking questions, the rods would cross for "yes" and stay still for "no." Apparently, while I was out of the building, the entity made its presence known to everyone else, specifically Kim. She told me later that she had seen it in her head and that it was not human. When she came running up the stairs, she said she had felt like it was attacking her and she had to get out. Some questions had been asked that, apparently, the entity did not like and its payback was to harass Kim and make her feel extremely unwelcome. She later told me that she felt like she was being stalked by something, that is was lurking around every corner in the room, waiting for its chance to attack.

The entity she described that appeared in her mind was truly frightening. Kim described it as "a tall thin being with long, gangly arms and legs." The "being" had large, dark eyes, but no mouth. After we left the building and were standing outside, another team psychic called to tell us to be careful. Even though she was not on the investigation that night, she had sensed the danger we were in while being over one-hundred miles away. She called and told us that what we were interacting with did not have good intentions. She then gave us the name of what she felt was harassing us. It was a demon. I will not repeat its name here in this story—not because I think it will manifest itself or do any harm, but because you just never know.

We decided to go back into the library, but before we did, we all said a little prayer of protection. Even Paul, who is an atheist thought "better safe than sorry," and joined in. Upon entering the basement, we immediately felt it, nothing. Whatever had been there just a short time ago was now gone. The feelings of dread, the uneasiness, and the thick air were all gone. Now, it was just a library

I will never be able to fully get my mind around what happened to us that night. Ghosts are much easier to accept then evil entities. Was there really a demonic presence with us that night? I will never be able to say for sure, but what I do know is this: If one believes in God, then that person must also accept the reality of the Devil and his minions. That night has changed me. I had never felt like that before, nor have I experienced anything even remotely close to that since. I sometimes worry that "it" will find me. That because I had seen it trying to appear, I am somehow "marked." I am not sure how rational that is, but every night before I go to sleep I do something now that I have not done for many years: I pray.

Smackover is a small town in south Arkansas. To get there, take I-530 south out of Little Rock to Exit 10. At this point, take US 167 south to El Dorado. Just before getting to El Dorado, turn back north on AR 7 toward Camden. This road will take you through the center of Smackover. The church-turned-Library/meeting room is in the center of town. They have haunted tours that are conducted on an as requested basis.

A Wild Ride

Arkansas State Capitol
Little Rock, Arkansas

The beauty of gleaming white halls, with polished brass hardware on ancient hardwood doors, of the Arkansas State Capitol can leave a person breathless. If one finds a time of day when the hustle and bustle of state business can be blocked out, they can hear the sounds of days gone by, and maybe even the voice of a friendly political ghost wishing them a good day.

The Arkansas State Capitol in Little Rock, Arkansas.

Early Arkansas politicians felt it necessary to build a new first-class building to house the territorial leaders of Arkansas. But before the building could be completed, the Arkansas Territory was voted in as a new state, so the territorial Capitol Building became the new State Capitol, and was soon embroiled in controversy.

The representatives settled differences by fighting on the house floor. In one instance, they settled their differences by fighting with knives, and this fight ended with the death of one of the representatives. Soon after the tragic knife fight, the South seceded from the Union and Arkansas voted, in the new building, to go to war. Once the war ended, Arkansas was accepted back into the Union, but debates and arguments delayed any healing legislative activity. In 1874, the newly elected governor was removed from office at gunpoint by his opponent. This revolution was called the Brooks/Baxter War; and federal troops were sent in to stop the attempted coup and restore order. The state was split by the election, and subsequent political fighting started anew. The political factions argued back and forth so much, the reconstruction years were not very constructive. From the beginning, the Capitol Building was filled with negative energy.

By the late 1800s, a movement was afoot to build a new State Capitol Building. Proponents stated that it would give the state a new start, and felt the old building had seen too many dark days. They believed that we, as a state, would never be able to heal and move forward unless a new building was constructed. Governor Daniel Jones suggested it be built on the existing state penitentiary grounds at Fifth Street. The site was level, with good drainage, and a great view of the river. In addition, Governor Jones thought the penitentiary sat on property that was too valuable for a prison, and "those kinds of people" should be housed away from the capital city. In 1899, the House voted to appropriate money to build a new State Capitol Building. The bill also included a section allowing the use of inmates to do the work.

George Mann was selected to draw the plans, and George Donaghey was selected to oversee construction. Construction of the foundations began in July of 1899; and it soon became obvious that the foundation was not going to be completed on time. The official cause of delay was weather; but, in fact, several unmarked graves were opened by the steam shovel digging the trenches. No one seemed to know that there were graves on the site, or who was buried there. Digging stopped while officials figured out what to do with the nine unwanted bodies. It is not known what happened to them.

Construction slowed to a crawl due to political allegations of fraud and shoddy craftsmanship. By 1905, work had virtually stopped on the Capitol Building. Most taxpayers were sold on the idea that it would never be completed unless the current politicians were removed from the process. Donaghey, the former Capitol Commissioner, decided the people were right. In 1908, he ran for governor with the promise that, if elected, he would see to it the new building was completed. This platform ensured him of a win, because taxpayers were tired of seeing their money wasted. Once in office, Donaghey fired the architect and the contractor. He hired new people and started back to work in earnest. Under a blanket of lawsuits and accusations, the new Capitol Building was occupied in December of 1910. There were still a few minor items that needed to be finished while business was conducted, and it took five more years to complete the construction as designed.

In the end, the new State Capitol Building became a centerpiece of political power. It stands 440 feet long, 195 feet wide, and 213 feet tall with neoclassical details. Like most other statehouses at the time, it was laid out in the shape of a cross with a sparkling white dome topped with a gold-covered cupola. The inside of the building is just as impressive. The walls and staircases are made of white marble and office walls are covered with polished oak panels. Highly polished brass was used for all of the hardware on the doors and lighting.

At night, when the lights go out and the employees are gone for the day, it is said that shadowy figures lurk in the dark recesses waiting for unsuspecting visitors or late night workers to harass.

An investigative photo taken in one of the council rooms. The bright spot in the upper right is believed to be a very active energy orb. *Photo courtesy of Spirit Seekers Paranormal Investigation Research and Intervention Team (SPIRIT).*

Locked In

When I was very young, my parents used to take me and my siblings to town to see the Christmas lights. One year, we went to see the lights at the State Capitol and, while we were there, we went to look at the different Christmas trees displayed inside the Capitol Building. I only remember bits and pieces of this family outing; but the most vivid memory of that night was fear. The fact that the Capitol was big with vast open areas that were dimly lit gave the inside of the building a feeling of gloom. Back in those days, the Capitol was not guarded twenty-four hours a day, but was locked up at night. The hours of operation were clearly stated on the doors, but when we went in, the doors were propped open making it impossible to read visiting hours posted on the sign.

The family was inside looking around and closing time came and went. Once we started to leave, we found all of the doors locked and no one inside to help us get out. We wandered around from door to door, hoping to find one unlocked or maybe a security guard on the outside who could open up and let us out.

I love my Dad, but he could be mischievous. When he saw the doors were locked, barring our exit, he started telling ghost stories. One was about the ghost of a kindly old man thought to be one of our lawmakers, who had died in the building while walking down the long marble staircase leading to the exit

This photo was taken in the basement of the Capitol. The investigator was alone and in total darkness. The camera flash was blocked by a shadow spirit standing between her and the other wall, only six feet away. *Photo courtesy of Spirit Seekers Paranormal Investigation Research and Intervention Team (SPIRIT).*

doors. I do not know if it was the ghost of the legislator I saw that night so long ago, or if it was my young imagination, but as we were headed down the stairs to the exit, I saw a man in a suit wearing a derby. As he walked by us, he doffed his hat and smiled. I watched him walk by and Dad told me to turn around and watch where I was going. We finally found a way out, but ever since, I have been looking for the nice man on the staircase.

Inside the Capitol Building

Not long ago, I was given permission by the Office of the Secretary of State to conduct an investigation into supernatural activity in the Capitol Building. This was something never allowed before, and I was honored to be permitted to bring my team of paranormal investigators into the building to spend the night. At the time of the investigation, I knew little about any ghost stories other than my own personal encounter. One of the Capital Police officers mentioned that an elevator might be haunted, but did not tell us which one. He said it tended to operate on its own. They had elevator repairmen out many times to fix it, but could never find a reason for it to work the way it did. The guard told us if a door was open, it was open to us.

A Shadow

Since it was such a large building, I brought a group of eight investigators. We split into groups of four, and one group started on the top floor while the second began in the basement. Everyone went about taking pictures and setting up various tests in different areas of the building. I was called to the second floor about 9 p.m. to help one of the teams verify or debunk a possible encounter with a spirit. They had been getting abnormal temperature and electromagnetic readings. Usually, if the temperature swings ten degrees in either direction, we start looking for the cause. That is when we break out the EMF meter to check for unusually high electromagnetic readings. When both of these pieces of equipment are indicating high readings, it is commonly believed that the investigator is in the presence of a ghost.

We were close to the steps where I had seen the ghost of the kind old legislator when I was a kid, so I was hoping we were onto something. I took lots of pictures as the team trailed the cold spots from the top of the steps to the side rooms where it disappeared. As it turns out, one picture did seem to show an entity, as one of the investigators was smudged out of the picture. Everything else was in perfect focus, but he was covered by a dark blur. While reviewing pictures, I noticed one taken in the basement. The investigator reported feeling like someone was in the room with her, so she took a picture in the direction of some lockers. The picture showed us that she was not alone. There was a very clear shadow person in the room with her.

A Wild Ride

Later in the evening, the teams switched up a bit, and all of the ladies decided to go looking for proof of a haunting on their own. The guys were on the first floor when we heard a scream. Thinking the girls were simply having fun, we waited and did not immediately respond. The second scream sent us going up the stairs, and in different directions.

We found them on the freight elevator in the back of the building. They appeared to be riding the elevator from floor to floor. As they went by, we heard them yell, "Get us off of this elevator!" After a few trips up and down, the door finally opened and they were allowed to leave.

The elevator is a typical freight elevator that requires a person to operate it. The open button must be fully depressed until the door is open and the close button must be held until it is closed. The elevator will not move until a floor is selected. However, none of that happened. As the investigators entered the elevator, the door closed and they went up and down, stopping momentarily at different floors until the elevator decided to let them off. It was discovered later that a state legislator named Ira Gurley had been crushed to death by the doors on an elevator.

Was this his ghost trying to get their attention, and give them a wild ride they would never forget? During the uncontrollable elevator ride, my voice recorder was on, and recorded a sigh after one of the screams. It was as if a spirit was pronouncing its aggravation with all of the commotion.

Evidence Review

After the investigation, during the evidence review time, we found a very interesting EVP. During one of the EVP question and answer sessions, an investigator asks, "Can you tell us your name?" The answer came through clear as a bell, "Edward." Edward and Ira, among others, had made their presence known to us in a very clear way at the Arkansas State Capitol that evening.

We were all honored to be given this once-in-a-lifetime opportunity and are very thankful to the Governor and the Secretary of State for allowing us to visit with some of the ghosts who walk the halls of the State Capitol, waiting to tell their story to anyone who will listen.

The Arkansas State Capitol is located at Woodlane and Capitol Avenue in Little Rock.

Spirits at Unrest

The Old Sanatorium
Northwest, Arkansas

An old Sanatorium sits atop a hill on the southern end of a small town in Northwest Arkansas. For years, it was the primary hospital in the state for those infected individuals with the dreaded tuberculosis. Originally opening in 1910 to combat the rise of the disease and give the sick a place to convalesce, it saw nearly 70,000 patients before it closed in the early 1970s. By that time, several more buildings had been constructed, including the main hospital building. This part of the facility was opened in 1941 and housed over 500 patients. There is little doubt that the state-of-the-art facility saved hundreds of lives, but there were also many lives lost, and not all have left the rundown halls of this sanatorium.

An Investigation

In 2006, Spirit Seekers was called in to investigate the empty hospital building. Upon arriving at the site, we split up into teams; each team was responsible for a floor. There are four floors in the old hospital and a basement. The teams set off to conduct their investigation duties.

It was not long before one of the team members experienced something odd. A female investigator was walking the second floor and taking photos when she noticed the nurse call lights were coming on as she passed each room. She stopped and the lights stopped, until she started walking again. As soon as she would pass each room, the little orange light that signaled to a nurse that a patient needed assistance would light up, then turn off as she passed. This continued down the entire length of the hallway.

Unseen hands touched two male investigators less than an hour after the lighting incident. They were walking on the fourth floor when something brushed against one of the investigator's chest. Moments later, the second investigator felt something tug at his pant leg three times, as if something wanted to get his attention. This "toying" with the investigators by the spirits continued throughout the night. Many heard voices whispering in the dark as if the spirits of the deceased patients were discussing the people who were in their building.

One of the major incidents of the night happened around 11 p.m. Alan was on the fourth floor checking on the investigation teams when, suddenly, right in front of him, what looked like the shadowy outline of a person darted out of a room and ran across the hallway to another room. He immediately ran to where he had seen the shadow person go, but when he entered the room, it was empty.

If ghosts are the great mystery of the paranormal world then the shadow person is the enigma. No one knows for sure what they are or why they are

This is an exterior view of the Logan County TB Sanatorium. *Photo courtesy of Spirit Seekers Paranormal Investigation Research and Intervention Team (SPIRIT).*

here. They are most easily described as black humanoid-shaped figures that lack any facial features, but bear the perfect silhouette of a person. Shadow people are usually associated with a place that has seen great tragedy or suffering—both of which the hospital building had seen in spades.

Soon after Alan experienced his sighting of a shadow person, another investigator was able to catch one on camera. The tall blacked-out silhouette was leaning against a wall, as if he were just standing there watching the investigators coming. It is highly unusual to capture one on film. On this night, at least it seemed the shadow people were out to play and did not mind if we saw them. All throughout the night there were sightings of them wandering the halls of different floors or darting from room to room. There is no way to know how many were in the building that night. It is quite possible that there was only one and it was jumping from floor to floor to watch *us* try and watch *it*.

A Follow-Up

On a follow-up investigation in 2007, we found more activity. A female investigator had been walking around the fifth floor with her team when she felt like she was being stalked. She stopped and took several photos. Upon inspecting the photos there was the face of man peering through a window in a door. All investigators were accounted for and when the room was inspected, all that was found were a couple of bird skeletons.

Shortly after this incident, two other female investigators were in the basement, and while conducting an EMF sweep they heard the voice of a woman. They could not quite make out what she was saying. The voice was mumbled and sounded as if it was far away. As they investigated the basement, the voice persisted, but no source was ever found.

The final incident happened just a few minutes before midnight. An investigator was on the third floor, alone. When she came to Room 332, she immediately felt as if someone was with her. She stood, looking around, thinking another investigator had come upstairs and was walking up behind her. There was nobody there. When she turned back towards the room, she saw the outline of a person standing not ten feet from where she stood. The apparition was not fully formed. The investigator could make out the upper part of the body, torso, arms, and head, but the form had no facial features and looked as if it was in mid-manifestation, and was either trying to appear or disappear. As she looked at the being, she began to feel physically ill. Her stomach started to cramp and her head began to ache. Moments later, the apparition completely disappeared and the investigator began feeling better the moment it was gone.

Before closing down the investigation for the night, Alan decided to try to make contact with a spirit by using dowsing rods. He started on the fifth floor and soon made contact. An answering system using *yes* and *no* was established. If the rods crossed, it was a *yes*; if they didn't move, that would be a *no*. After asking several questions, it was determined that the spirit wanted the team to go down to the fourth floor. Once the team was on the fourth floor, the spirit guided Alan to what it claimed was her room while she was a patient at the hospital.

Through a series of questions, the spirit claimed to have been a woman in her mid-forties. She was married and had one child before she died in the sanatorium of tuberculosis. She said she stayed at the old hospital because she liked it there, although she claimed there were many evil spirits in the building as well. Through the dowsing rods, she told Alan and the group that the evil spirits that inhabited the hospital mostly stayed on the third floor.

This is an interesting point, primarily because the third floor is where the prisoner lock-up area is located. Oftentimes, the hospital had to treat prisoners and individuals who had mental illnesses. When these types of patients were admitted, they were kept at the far end of the building, on the third floor away from other patients. A cage-like wall, replete with a locking door closed off the last four rooms at the end of the hall.

Contact with the female spirit broke off shortly after she told the team about the evil spirits in the building. The team tried for several minutes to reestablish contact without success. This exchange was caught on video and was recorded on several different audio devices. Soon after, the team packed up their gear and didn't return until 2008.

Third Time's a Charm

The third time Spirit Seekers investigated the sanatorium was just as active as the previous two investigations. Before the team arrived, Alan and I attempted to make contact with the woman that had been conversing with the group through the dowsing rods the year before. After several minutes of trying, our efforts paid off, and contact was established. As we had done the previous year, we asked several *yes* or *no* questions using the same protocols.

This questioning led us to the question: "What is your name?" The only way this could be answered was to tediously go through each letter of the alphabet and have the spirit cross the dowsing rods when we got to the correct letter. This session lasted nearly an hour as we rattled off each letter of the alphabet, waiting for a *yes* signal.

The spirit told us her name was Enid Lewis, and the reason she left us so quickly the year before was that the "evil ones" were coming and would punish her for contacting us. The only way to protect herself was to get away from them and us as fast as she could. We decided it would be best to leave Enid alone for the night. Angering evil entities was the last thing we wanted to do.

The activity started early on this investigation. Most people think spirits only come out when it is dark; this is not the case. Spirits can show themselves whenever they choose, day or night. We had one investigator walking the first floor taking baseline EMF and temperature readings. As she was making her way down the hallway, a nurse in a white uniform crossed the hall twenty feet in front of her. The investigator ran to the room where she had seen the nurse enter and found the door locked. The ghostly caregiver had simply walked through a solid oak door and disappeared.

On this night, it seemed the shadow people were particularly active. Four different investigators reported seeing the dark beings throughout the night. The thing that was different about the shadow people this night was that they varied in height. One investigator stated that he witnessed one dart across a hallway no more than ten feet in front of him. He also claimed that it was no more than four feet tall. All of the shadow people that had previously been sighted at the sanatorium had been average height.

Several investigators also heard the voices of children throughout the night. Many reported that they would hear giggling and whispering behind them only to turn around and see nothing but an empty hallway. Several investigators were understandably shaken by the fact that there were spirits of children in the sanatorium. It weighed heavy on our hearts and minds, especially when one thinks about what Enid told us about the evil spirits in the building. We said a short prayer and hoped the children would find peace.

Of the dozens of investigations Spirit Seekers has conducted, none offers the experience of the Old State Sanatorium. The tragedy, pain, and feelings of despair that permeate the hospital building lay heavy upon one's soul. As a person walks down the corridors where so many took their last breaths on this earth, I can tell you from first-hand experience: It was an extremely humbling, and eerie feeling.

This is an investigative photo taken on the fifth floor of the old Sanatorium. The investigator had heard her name whispered behind her just before taking this picture. She had no idea that there was a disembodied spirit looking at her through the window. *Photo courtesy of Spirit Seekers Paranormal Investigation Research and Intervention Team (SPIRIT).*

CONCLUSION

From the Dueling Grounds at West Memphis to the battlefields of the Boston Mountains to the haunted churches in the oil rich south, Arkansas's haunted history and heritage is deeply grounded in the beliefs and cultures of its people and places. The diverse cultural background of the state is a breeding ground for rich legends and lore. The stories that have been presented to you in *Supernatural Arkansas: Ghosts, Monsters and the Unexplained* are but a few of the haunted stories that supernatural enthusiasts will find as they travel the highways and byways of Arkansas.

Thank you for joining us on our supernatural adventure.

LOCATION INDEX